Around the World
with Wendy and Barb

Around the World with Wendy and Barb

More Great-Tasting, Low-Fat Recipes from the Authors of *Spread Yourself Thin*

HarperCollins*Publishers*Ltd

http://www.harpercanada.com

Writers and Researchers: Lori Richmond/Lynn Waters
Photographer: Joseph Marranca Photography
Food Stylist: Mara Subotincic
Props Stylists: Mary Kotsopoulos/Carol Gall
Props generously donated or loaned by Bowring (Mississauga), Pier 1 (Oakville),
The Bay (Oakville), Stokes (Burlington), Sunveil Sunwear (Oakville),
and Bay King Motors (Hamilton).

HarperCollins books may be purchased for educational, business, or sales promotional use.
For information please write: Special Markets Department, HarperCollins Canada,
55 Avenue Road, Suite 2900, Toronto, Ontario, Canada M5R 3L2

First edition

Canadian Cataloguing in Publication Data

Buckland, Wendy
Around the world with Wendy and Barb: more great-tasting,
low-fat recipes from the authors of Spread yourself thin

Includes index.
ISBN 0-00-638548-6

1. Low-fat diet – Recipes. 2. Cookery, International.
I. Nicoll, Barb. II Title.

RM237.7.B824 1999   641.5′638   C99-930444-5

99 00 01 02 03 04 WEB 6 5 4 3 2 1

Printed and bound in Canada

My darling Don,
My true friend & inspiration,
for what you encourage me to do, and to be.
I respect your example, your deeds, and ideas.
With much love.

Always, Wendy

To
John
I can't tell you how lucky
I am to have met you . . . .
I love you.

Jake
Every day, every night
I thank God for you.

And special thanks for so much
to my parents, Bud and Rose.

—Barb

Contents

Introduction

Come on board the Wendy and Barb Express. This is your ticket to travel the world through international cuisine. If this is your introduction to us, Wendy and Barb, we're glad you've joined us. We guarantee you will be transported to the ends of the globe through our international recipes. If you know us at all, you've heard of our struggles with life's challenges, including weight loss. You know that we both love to eat. You also know that we have drastically changed our lifestyles so that, by using a low-fat approach, we can enjoy the foods we want. Between the two of us, we have lost over 103 pounds! Not an easy thing to do when juggling jobs, kids, families and other personal challenges. You have been writing and faxing us, asking for another book. We are happy to say, here it is!

We have traveled from Victoria to Halifax via T.V., radio and personal appearances to promote our last cookbook, *Spread Yourself Thin.* For Barb, who had never been farther from her hometown of Toronto than northern Ontario, that tour was doubly exciting. For both of us, it was an opportunity unlike any other to speak and, most importantly, to listen to our fans. We have been called "Canadian inspirations." This has touched us more than you will ever know.

When we were traveling, promoting our book, we met and shared recipes and tears with men and women from all walks of life. This great country of ours became much smaller. In fact, the whole world seemed to become a lot smaller. Living in Canada allows us to indulge in many delicious foods. We discovered that we could easily transport ourselves to any country in the world if we embraced the culture, including the cuisine, of that country. We didn't have to be in Italy to enjoy traditional Italian food. We thought that you too would love to be transported to other countries through the art of cooking. So, that's what we have done. We wanted another fun cookbook filled with delicious recipes that everyone can enjoy. With a little effort and a little time in the grocery store, you can escape from the typical North American dishes (although, if you're anything like us, you love a burger with fries on occasion). With this cookbook, we've taken recipes for dishes from around the world and made them delicious and low-fat. Now everyone can enjoy some Mediterranean Magic without having to spend a fortune on travel. Did you know that pumpkin soup is a favorite in Australia? Well, now you do, and we provide just the recipe. We've even come up with a couple of buffets for simple but sophisticated dinners. Also, we've included an After-Theater New York Cocktail Party, for those party-goers like us. To close each chapter, we've sent you postcards from our travels, brimming with valuable information you can use in the kitchen and tips for a healthier — both physically and mentally — lifestyle.

As you may know, we don't diet; we just make sure that we keep our daily intake of fat at less than 30% of our calorie intake. When we were losing weight, we would have loved to have had cookbooks like *Spread Yourself Thin* or *Around the World:* lively and informative cookbooks written by people who have struggled with weight and weight loss. And if only someone had created a line of low-fat food products back then. We know that our You Won't Believe This is Low-Fat products have helped thousands of you keep weight off by sticking to your low-fat intakes. We applaud you. If you persevere, it is possible to stay under that 30% mark. We know that sometimes it is difficult, but in the end, it's so worth it! Don't forget, we struggle too. In our first book, *Armed and Dangerous,* we talked a lot about our personal struggles with life and weight loss. We also stressed the importance of fitness and exercise. If you remember Wendy's story, exercise and weight training changed her life. We know that when things get rough, it's difficult to stick to an exercise program and to be careful what you eat. You want to curl up on the couch with comfort food. But exercising isn't just about keeping trim. We do it for mental and emotional release, too. We believe that you can't lose weight and *not* be mentally and emotionally healthier. Watching what we eat and exercising is the key to our success. We believed in it and it worked. We hope it's working for you or that, with this book, you will now let it work for you.

And now we want to update you on what we've been up to since our last book.

Wendy's Story: Preparing to write this book gave me an opportunity to collect my thoughts and fond memories of the past year. Thanks to our tour across Canada, Barb and I were able to meet and share experiences with many of you who had written us. I am extremely moved that our stories of our personal struggles with weight loss have so touched you. We have had a lot of positive feedback on the book and we appreciate it very much. I feel privileged now to be able to share with you recipes from around the world, recipes we have collected either from friends made during our travels or those created in our home kitchens.

My most memorable and touching experience during the tour is that of a 40ish-year-old woman, visibly flushed, moving towards me with great speed in an Edmonton grocery store. She came up to me at the demonstration booth and gave me a bone-crushing hug. She burst into tears and tried to express herself, but was unable to. I was extremely confused and a little concerned. I didn't know this woman, and I mistook her happiness for sadness. But she was hugging me to thank me. Barb and I had touched her. She told us that for the first time in her life, she was energetic, well adjusted and happy. She was half the weight she was 18 months ago. She continued to tell us that we were her inspirations through our personal stories and suggestions for food preparations. Our helpful hints on activities and exercising had turned her life around. I was so happy for her, I burst into tears. At that moment, I realized that sharing my pain could actually help others. When Barb and I began our journey, we really had no idea of the impact we would have on others. We are very happy to have helped you in any way we have.

Barb's Story: Since the release of *Spread Yourself Thin,* my life has changed dramatically. Looking back, I realize the book had something to do with it. Whenever I look at or think about that book, I feel independent and stand proud. When I was overweight, which had been most of my life, I didn't have a lot of courage or self-esteem. I was not true to myself. Writing and researching the book was the catalyst I needed to make some major changes in my life. I lost weight, ate healthily and exercised not only my body but also my mind. My son Jake (3 1/2 years old at the time) and I started on a new journey. I've never looked back and I just keep gaining steam. Jake and I are quite a team. We are enjoying life to the fullest, experimenting with new projects. I am no longer afraid of life's challenges. My positive attitude and peace of mind seem to radiate off my son. So my journey now is that of an independent, single mother who is happy to be living life with no regrets. I am happy when I think of how far I have come.

I loved doing the book tour and traveling across Canada; it was absolutely thrilling. Thank you all for your support. Every time someone comes up to me, or writes to say that he or she has taken up running just as I did, I have to smile. Those who have added a marathon or a public run to your exercise program, I cheer you. The marathon I ran was more than just a sports race to me. Apart from becoming a mother, it was the first time I felt I had accomplished something great. More importantly, I did it just for me. For those of you exercising, I am delighted that you are exercising towards a better you.

Again, we would both like to say thank you to our fans, who have given us the opportunity to write another book. Nothing makes us happier than to let our creative imaginations run wild, especially when it comes to food. From the classics of Canada to the allure of Asia, we know that you will love our international tour. Welcome aboard. Fasten your seatbelts, and enjoy the ride around the world with Wendy and Barb!

Chapter 1

Canadian Classics

East Coast Lobster Party

Bluenose Brown Bread
Grilled Lobster with Tri-Dipping Sauces
Cabot Trail Corn
P.E.I. Pesto Potato Salad
Oatmeal Chocolate Chip Cookies

Quebec Lunch for Four

Fiddlehead Soup
Frizzy Frisée and Wild Mushroom Salad
Toasted Bagels with Herbed Yogo Cheese and Arctic Char
Wild Blueberries with Maple Cream

Muskoka Barbeque

Dillyicious Cucumber Salad
Cedar Plank Salmon
Veggie Kebobs
Herbed Baked Potatoes
Flim Flam Fruit Flan
Canadian Coffee

How the West Was Won

Okanagan Peach Daiquiris
Carrot-Ginger Vichyssoise
Alberta Peppercorn Steak
Rodeo Rice
Saskatoon Berries with Fromage Blanc

Canada. Our home and native land. We thought it appropriate to begin our world adventure here at home. Whether you live in Charlottetown or Victoria or somewhere in between, these menus will allow you to enjoy some classic recipes that we and our friends across Canada hold dear and consider delicious. What's even better is that it's all low-fat, simple, easy cooking. From the rocky mountains of British Columbia, the plains of the Prairies, the lakes of Ontario and the raw beauty of the East, Canada's diversity offers us much to choose from. We Canadians are fortunate to have an abundant choice of vegetables and fruits. The recipes in this book are regional, so we use produce from local markets whenever possible. If you don't have access to specific vegetables and fruits called for in these recipes (for example, Okanagan peaches or saskatoon berries), don't worry, we've given you alternatives that will not compromise the fat/calorie content of the dishes.

We stand on guard and salute our native land for its greatness. We stand and salute you for taking up the fight against fat and for a healthy lifestyle. Keep reading for a little taste of our home. We begin our cross-Canada tour on the East Coast with a lobster party, complete with Grilled Lobster with Tri-Dipping Sauces, Cabot Trail Corn and P.E.I. Pesto Potato Salad. Pull out those shell crackers and newspapers, play some Great Big Sea or Cape Breton Barbarians to set the mood, roll up your sleeves and have lots of fun. Picnic tables are a must. As well, we suggest paper plates for an easy clean-up.

A tour of Quebec would be pointless without a stop in old Quebec City. The history and magic of the historic city are captured in our recipes. A great lunch or brunch of Fiddlehead Soup, Toasted Bagels with Herbed Yogo Cheese and Arctic Char and Wild Blueberries with Maple Cream is a great indulgence after a long walk on the cobblestone, and a great substitute for those fatty comfort foods we love on those cold, wintery days.

Summer getaways to the Muskokas, or any lake nearby, is as much a part of us as is our battle with fat. Summer barbeques are something we look forward to on those cold, wintery nights. In the summer, we love to take full advantage of fresh salmon, summer cucumbers and freshly picked dill. The menu, including Cedar Plank Salmon and Veggie Kebobs, is our perfect summer cottage or backyard feast. Don't forget that after-dinner walk on the beach or catching the sunset on the dock while you enjoy a flavorful Canadian Coffee.

A Canadian tour would be incomplete without visiting the West Coast. We've included recipes for a mouth-watering Carrot-Ginger Vichyssoise as well as for Grade A Alberta beef. Do we spoil ourselves or what? We weren't kidding when we said that we love scrumptious, low-fat dishes. We hope you enjoy our Canadian favorites as much as we do. There's more to Canadian cuisine than back bacon and beer, eh?

Menu 1

East Coast Lobster Party

Bluenose Brown Bread
Grilled Lobster with Tri-Dipping Sauces
Cabot Trail Corn
P.E.I. Pesto Potato Salad
Oatmeal Chocolate Chip Cookies

Wine Suggestions

Peller Estates Oakridge Chardonnay, Ontario

For Beer Lovers

A down-east tradition, Alexander Keith's Pale Ale, celebrating its 125th anniversary this year.

Bluenose Brown Bread

Makes 2 loaves
(16 slices each)

Per serving
(1 slice):

Calories: 98
Fat: 0.7g

Do you love bread half as much as we do? Here's a low-fat, tasty alternative to the fat-laden stuff offered at most grocery stores. Remember, though, this is homemade bread without preservatives, so try to eat it right away. (We don't think you'll have any problem with that last instruction.)

> 1 cup (250 mL) quick-cooking oats
> 1 tsp (5 mL) salt
> 1 tbsp (15 mL) margarine
> 1/2 cup + 1 tsp (125 mL + 5mL) molasses
>   (divided)
> 2 cups (500 mL) boiling water
> 1 package (1/4 oz/8 g) active dry yeast
> 1/2 cup (125 mL) lukewarm water
> 5 to 6 cups (1.25 to 1.5 L) all-purpose flour

Combine the oats, salt, margarine and 1/2 cup (125 mL) of the molasses in a large mixing bowl. Add the boiling water and stir until well combined. Set aside to cool.

In a small bowl, stir together the remaining 1 teaspoon (5 mL) molasses and 1/2 cup (125 mL) lukewarm water. Sprinkle the yeast over the top of the water and stir to dissolve the yeast. Let stand until mixture becomes foamy, about 5 minutes. Add it to the oat mixture and combine. Add the flour, 1 cup (250 mL) at a time, and stir until fully incorporated into the oat mixture.

Turn the dough out onto a floured board and knead until smooth, about 5 minutes. Shape the dough into a ball and place in a large bowl. Cover with waxed paper that has been sprayed with non-stick cooking spray and let rise in a warm place free from drafts until the dough has doubled in bulk, about 1 hour. Punch dough down and remove from bowl. Divide the dough in half and shape into two loaves. Place each loaf into a 9x5-inch (2 L) loaf pan that has been sprayed with non-stick cooking spray. Cover again and let rise 1 more hour.

Preheat oven to 350° (180° C). Bake the loaves for 30 to 40 minutes. Remove from pans and let cool on wire rack.

Postcards from the Edge

In the Kitchen

Cows have been bred leaner over the last 10 years than ever before. Still, trim as much fat from the beef as you can before cooking it. Beef is rich in iron, zinc and B-vitamins. Try to keep portion sizes around 3 to 5 ounces (90 to 150 g).

You can always substitute vegetable stock for chicken stock. It tastes very similar and reduces the overall fat content. If you don't have the time to make your own stock, some very good ones are available in the grocery store. Just remember to look for the low-fat brands.

Whenever a recipe calls for oil for sautéing, you can substitute de-fatted chicken or vegetable stock. We do use small amounts of oil and non-stick cookware, but if you'd like go one step farther, try using stock instead.

Salmon contains naturally occurring fats called omega-3 fatty acids. Studies have shown that these fats may help prevent blood clots, which are the major cause of heart attack. They have also been shown to lower cholesterol levels. Tuna, trout, bluefish, mackerel and sardines are also great sources of omega-3s.

Grilled Lobster with Tri-Dipping Sauces

Serves 6

Per serving:

Calories: 135
Fat: 1.4 g

Try to use mesquite wood on the barbeque — it gives the lobsters a very sweet-smoky taste and is readily available at specialty food stores. To serve lobsters in a real East Coast fashion, simply cover your dining table or picnic table with sheets of newspaper and put the grilled lobsters in the middle. The only other things you'll need are shell crackers and lots of napkins. For a quick clean up, simply roll up the newspaper with all of the discarded shells inside and the dishes are done.

6 live lobsters, about 1 lb (500 g) each

Fill a very large stockpot with enough water to cover the lobsters (you may have to boil them 2 or 3 at a time) and bring the water to a rolling boil. Put lobsters, head first, into the water (this will kill them immediately). Cook for 4 minutes. Remove lobsters, pat dry and set aside.

Preheat barbeque to medium-high heat with the grill 8 inches (20 cm) from the heat source. Grill the lobsters for 5 minutes, then turn and cook another 5 to 7 minutes with the barbeque lid down.

Put the lobsters in the middle of the newspaper-covered table and serve with the following dipping sauces.

Dipping Sauces
for Lobster

Our Lemon Dill Dip is the perfect substitute for butter; we use de-fatted chicken stock for a rich, drippy delight. Want something with a little kick? How about our homemade Cocktail Sauce with just a bite of horseradish? And for a creamy, dreamy finish, we offer you our Creamy Mustard Dip with a hint of fresh tarragon.

Lemon Dill Dip

**Makes 1 cup
(250 mL)**

**Per serving
(2 tbsp/30 mL):**

**Calories: 18
Fat: 0.2 g**

2/3 cup (150 mL) de-fatted chicken, fish or
   vegetable stock
2 tbsp (25 mL) lemon juice
2 tsp (10 mL) sugar
grated zest of 1/2 a lemon
2 tbsp (25 mL) snipped fresh dill

Mix all ingredients in a small saucepan and heat over medium heat until just warmed through. Remove from heat and serve. If possible, keep the sauce warm by setting the serving dish over a tealight candle.

Cocktail Sauce

2/3 cup (150 mL) chili sauce
2 tbsp (25 mL) lemon juice
2 tsp (10 mL)horseradish
1 clove garlic, finely minced

**Makes 1 cup
(250 mL)**

**Per serving
(2 tbsp/30 mL):**

**Calories: 4
Fat: 0 g**

Mix all ingredients together in a small bowl. Refrigerate until ready to serve.

Creamy Mustard Dip

1/2 cup (125 mL) non-fat sour cream
1 tbsp (15 mL) Dijon or hot mustard
1 tsp (5 mL) cider vinegar
2 tbsp (25 mL) chopped fresh tarragon, or 1 tbsp
  (15 mL) dried tarragon
3 tbsp (45 mL) skim milk

**Makes 1 cup
(250 mL)**

**Per serving
(2 tbsp/30 mL):**

**Calories: 25
Fat: 0.1 g**

Mix sour cream, mustard, vinegar and tarragon in a small bowl. Add milk, 1 tablespoon (15 mL) at a time, until you reach the desired dipping consistency. Refrigerate until ready to serve.

Cabot Trail Corn

Nothing else compares to the first corn of the summer. When it's young and fresh, and grilled using our method, there is really no need for copious amounts of butter. You may want to indulge in a small amount of butter, but we suggest you take a bite of the corn first. The sweet, roasted taste is heaven all on its own.

6 ears fresh, unshucked corn
large bucket of cold water, with 1 tbsp (15 mL)
  salt added
salt and fresh ground pepper to taste

Put the unshucked corn into the bucket of salted water and let sit for 2 hours. Remove corn and pat dry. Carefully pull back outer husks of corn, being careful not to remove from stem. Remove all of the silk from the corn and pull the husks back over the corn to cover.

Preheat the barbeque to medium-high, with the grill 8 inches (20 cm) from the heat source. Cook the corn on the barbeque for 20 to 30 minutes, with the barbeque lid down. Turn the corn occasionally so that grill marks on the corn husks are even.

To serve, peel back a small amount of the husks at the top of the ear to show some of the cob. Season with salt and pepper to taste.

P.E.I. Pesto Potato Salad

Serves 6

Per serving:
Calories: 111
Fat: 1.4 g

No run-of-the-mill potato salad for us girls. Hold the mayo. Hold the oil. A fresh, low-fat pesto takes the place of the usual dressing that accompanies most potato salads.

> 1 1/2 lb (700 g) new red potatoes, each the size of
>   a golf ball, about 18
> 1/2 cup (125 mL) chopped red peppers
> 2 green onions, sliced, for garnish
>
> Pesto:
> 1 cup (250 mL) basil leaves, loosely packed
> 1/3 cup (75 mL) de-fatted chicken or vegetable
>   stock
> 1/4 cup (50 mL) grated Parmesan cheese
> 1 tbsp (15 mL) toasted pine nuts
> 1 to 2 cloves garlic, peeled
> 1/4 tsp (1 mL) salt

Scrub potatoes and put in a saucepan, adding just enough water to cover. Bring to a boil and cook until tender, about 20 minutes. Add the red pepper to the potatoes for the last 1 minute of cooking. Drain and set aside to cool.

While potatoes are cooking, put all of the pesto ingredients in a food processor or blender. Blend until smooth.

Cut each potato in half and put in a large bowl with the red peppers. Add just enough pesto to coat potatoes and toss. Garnish with green onion and serve.

**Makes about
14 cookies**

**Per serving
(1 cookie):**

**Calories: 141
Fat: 2.5 g**

Oatmeal Chocolate Chip Cookies

The oats in these cookies reflect the Scottish influence in Maritime cooking. Since Wendy is of Scottish descent (and a cookie monster), these simple but satisfying cookies hold a special place in her heart (and tummy).

1 1/2 cups (375 mL) large-flake oats
1 cup (250 mL) all-purpose flour or whole wheat
   pastry flour
1/2 tsp (2 mL) baking soda
1/2 tsp (2 mL) baking powder
1/2 cup (125 mL) brown sugar
1/2 cup (125 mL) unsweetened applesauce
1/4 cup (50 mL) honey or light corn syrup
1 egg white, beaten
1 tsp (5 mL) vanilla extract
1/2 cup (125 mL) chocolate chips

Preheat oven to 350°F (180°C).

Combine the oats, flour, baking soda and baking powder in a small mixing bowl. Stir to combine and set aside. In a large mixing bowl, combine the sugar, applesauce, honey, egg white and vanilla extract. Mix well. Add the dry ingredients to the applesauce mixture and mix well. Stir in the chocolate chips.

Using a 1/4 cup (50 mL) measure, scoop portions of the dough onto an ungreased parchment-lined baking sheet, leaving a 1 1/2- to 2-inch (4 to 5 cm) space between cookies. Flatten each cookie slightly and bake until nicely browned at edges, about 12 to 15 minutes. Remove and allow to cool slightly on cookie sheet. Transfer cookies to a wire rack to cool completely.

Postcards from the Edge

Living a Healthy Lifestyle

When you want to go out walking, speed walking or hiking, team up with a friend. Doing so will help you stick to your routine as well as motivate you. Choose someone who has the same goals as you so that you can share in your accomplishments.

Alberta and British Columbia boast some of the greatest skiing areas in the world. Since skiing is both an expensive and physically challenging sport, why not rent equipment for the day and take a lesson on one of the smaller hills to see if you like it? Cross-country skiing is also a tremendous calorie-fat burner. Winter is no excuse to curl up under a blanket and eat Twinkies in front of the T.V. Get out there and enjoy to the fullest all of the seasons our great country has to offer.

Menu 2

Quebec Lunch for Four

Fiddlehead Soup
Frizzy Frisée and Wild Mushroom Salad
Toasted Bagels with Herbed Yogo Cheese and Arctic Char
Wild Blueberries with Maple Cream

Wine Suggestions

Jackson Triggs, Riesling Dry, V.Q.A., Ontario

Fiddlehead Soup

Serves 4

Per serving:

Calories: 83
Fat: 2.2 g

Fiddleheads are a springtime treat, for they have an extremely short season. Although frozen fiddleheads are available year round, save this recipe for when you can buy them fresh. Or, you can substitute fresh chopped asparagus for the fiddleheads.

> 2 tsp (10 mL) margarine
> 1 lb (500 g) fiddleheads, washed well and tails
>   trimmed
> 1 large potato, peeled and diced
> salt and pepper to taste
> 1 tbsp (15 mL) all-purpose flour
> 5 cups (1.25 L) de-fatted chicken stock
> juice of 1/2 lemon
> 1/4 tsp (1 mL) nutmeg
> 1 tsp (5 mL) dried chervil
> 1/4 cup (50 mL) skim milk

Melt the margarine in a large saucepan over medium heat. Add the fiddleheads and potato and sauté for 3 to 4 minutes. Season with salt and pepper. Sprinkle the flour over the mixture and stir to incorporate. Cook for 1 minute. Add stock, lemon juice, nutmeg and chervil. Cook over medium heat for 20 to 30 minutes.

Pass the soup through a food mill or process in a food processor or blender. Return the soup to the saucepan and add the milk. Slowly reheat, being careful not to boil.

Serves 4

Per serving:

Calories: 74
Fat: 2.4 g

Frizzy Frisée and Wild Mushroom Salad

Frisée is a crazy, curly endive with a bitter taste that accents the mushrooms in this recipe well. Use a mixture of wild mushrooms such as chanterelle, morel, cremini, oyster or small portobello. If these aren't available, simply substitute regular white mushrooms.

2 tsp (10 mL) olive oil
1 small onion, minced
1 clove garlic, finely minced
1 lb (500 g) wild mushrooms, cleaned and sliced
2 tsp (10 mL) chopped fresh thyme, or 1 tsp (5 mL) dried
2 tsp (10 mL) chopped fresh rosemary, or 1 tsp (5 mL) dried
3 tbsp (50 mL) chopped fresh parsley
1/4 cup (50 mL) red wine
salt and pepper to taste
1 small head of frisée, leaves separated, washed and dried
fresh thyme sprigs for garnish

Heat the oil in a large non-stick skillet. Add the onion and garlic and sauté over medium heat for 3 minutes. Add the mushrooms and sauté until they begin to release their juices, about 5 minutes. Add the thyme, rosemary, parsley and wine and turn heat up to high. Cook, stirring occasionally, until most of the liquid has evaporated, about 10 minutes. Season with salt and pepper.

Place frisée leaves on 4 serving plates and top each with some of the mushroom mixture, pouring a little of the remaining juice over each serving. Garnish with fresh thyme sprigs.

Toasted Bagels with Herbed Yogo Cheese and Arctic Char

Serves 4

Per serving:
Calories: 198
Fat: 2.4 g

This is the first recipe in this book in which we suggest you use Yogo Cheese. This cheese has become an old friend of ours on our path to a low-fat lifestyle. It is a versatile substitute for many ingredients that are high in fat, as you'll see throughout the book. Here we use it in place of high-fat cream cheese. Seasoned with fresh herbs and topped with the subtle, smoky flavor of the arctic char, Yogo Cheese on bagels is an elegant addition to our lunch.

2 plain bagels
3/4 cup (175 mL) Herbed Yogo Cheese (below)
8 thin slices smoked arctic char (1/4 lb/125 g
   total weight)
sliced lemon and whole chives for garnish

Herbed Yogo Cheese:
3/4 cup (175 mL) twice-drained Yogo Cheese
   (recipe follows)
1 tbsp (15 mL) snipped fresh dill
1 tbsp (15 mL) snipped fresh chives
2 tsp (10 mL) lemon juice

Slice the bagels in half evenly and lightly toast. While bagels toast, make the Herbed Yogo Cheese by mixing together the Yogo Cheese, dill, chives and lemon juice in a small bowl. Just before serving, spread Herbed Yogo Cheese on each bagel half. Top each with 2 slices of the arctic char. Garnish with sliced lemon and whole chives.

Yogo Cheese

2 cups (500 mL) plain non-fat yogurt

Put yogurt in a coffee-filter-lined colander set over a bowl and refrigerate. Let drain for 12 hours. Discard any liquid that accumulates in the bowl. For a firmer cheese, repeat process. Makes approximately 1 cup (250 mL).

๏๏ ๏๏ ๏๏ ๏๏ ๏๏ ๏๏ ๏๏ ๏๏ ๏๏ ๏๏ ๏๏ ๏๏ ๏๏ ๏๏ ๏๏ ๏๏ ๏๏ ๏๏

Postcards from the Edge

Just Remember

Even if you're on the right track, you'll get run over if you just sit there.
— Will Rogers

Now that you have the information on how to change your life in a positive way, put that info to work and set your plan in motion!

Wild Blueberries with Maple Cream

Serves 4

Per serving:
Calories: 133
Fat: 2.4 g

Since Quebec supplies the rest of Canada with about 90% of the maple syrup it consumes, we wanted to include it in one of our recipes. Try to get pure maple syrup — the artificially flavored syrup just can't compare. If you're preparing this menu in the late spring and live near a maple syrup farm, visit the farm in the morning to buy a small bottle of fresh maple syrup, then go back home and make this scrumptious lunch dessert.

> 1 pint (500 mL) wild blueberries, washed (rasp-
> berries, strawberries or other seasonal fruit may
> be substituted)
> 1 cup (250 mL) light whipped topping, thawed in
> refrigerator
> 2 tbsp (25 mL) pure maple syrup
> 1/2 cup (125 mL) non-fat sour cream
> lemon zest curls for garnish

Wash the berries and refrigerate until ready to use. Put the whipped topping in a small bowl and drizzle in the maple syrup. Stir gently to combine. Put sour cream in a medium-sized bowl. Gently fold the whipped topping into the sour cream.

Divide berries among 4 serving dishes and top each with the maple cream. Garnish with additional berries and a lemon zest curl. You could also layer the berries and maple cream in parfait glasses.

Menu 3

Muskoka Barbeque

Dillyicious Cucumber Salad
Cedar Plank Salmon
Veggie Kebobs
Herbed Baked Potatoes
Flim Flam Fruit Flan
Canadian Coffee

Wine Suggestions

Chateau des Charmes Pinot Noir, V.Q.A., Ontario

or

Chateau des Charmes Chardonnay, V.Q.A., Ontario

Dillyicious Cucumber Salad

Serves 6

Per serving:

Calories: 20
Fat: 0.2 g

Eeek. It's mid-summer and the cucumbers are taking over the garden. Pass them on to your neighbors, but be sure to save enough for this classic salad. It's a good idea to make more than you think you'll need. If you're like us, you'll have a hard time not dipping into the bowl every time you open the refrigerator.

> 2 medium cucumbers
> 1 bunch radishes
> 1/4 cup (50 mL) snipped fresh dill
> 3/4 cup (175 mL) vinegar
> 1/4 tsp (1 mL) salt
> 1 tsp (5 mL) sugar

Wash the cucumbers (but do not peel) and pat dry. Scrape the tines of a fork down the sides of each cucumber to create a ridged pattern. Slice cucumbers very thinly and put in a bowl. Wash and trim radishes, slice thinly and add to the cucumbers. Sprinkle dill over the cucumbers and radishes. Combine the vinegar, salt and sugar and pour over the vegetables. Refrigerate for at least 1 hour to let the flavors combine.

Cedar Plank Salmon

Although this recipe calls for an unusual method of preparation, once the aroma of the cedar on the barbeque starts to fill the air, not only are you well on your way to creating a delicious entrée, you have also created an ambiance your guests won't easily forget. Cedar planks are available at your local hardware store.

3 untreated cedar planks (each 1 inch/2.5 cm thick)
6 salmon steaks, approximately 5 oz (150 g) each

Marinade:
1/4 cup (50 mL) teriyaki sauce
1/4 cup (50 mL) orange juice
2 tbsp (25 mL) brown sugar
1 tbsp (15 mL) fresh ginger, grated

Soak the cedar planks in water overnight or for at least 3 hours, weighing them down with a couple of dinner plates so they stay submerged.

Mix together the marinade ingredients in a shallow glass dish. Coat the salmon steaks with the marinade, turning as necessary. Refrigerate for 1 hour.

Pat the cedar planks dry and place 2 of the salmon steaks on each plank. Preheat barbeque to medium-high heat with grill 8 inches (20 cm) from the heat source. Place the salmon on planks on the grill and cook for 10 to 15 minutes, with the barbeque lid down. Turn the steaks once. The salmon will be cooked when it is just opaque and flakes easily when tested with a fork. Check the salmon often so you don't overcook it.

Veggie Kebobs

Serves 6

Per serving:
Calories: 138
Fat: 2.4 g

Although we've suggested certain veggies to use for the kebobs, take a trip to the local farmers' market and let the abundant array of freshly picked vegetables be your guide. Remember, the fresher the vegetables, the more nutrients they have.

> 6 metal or wooden skewers (if using wooden skewers, presoak in warm water for 1 hour so they don't burn on the barbeque)
> 1 yellow pepper, seeded and cut in 1-inch (2.5 cm) chunks
> 1 green pepper, seeded and cut in 1-inch (2.5 cm) chunks
> 2 red onions, cut in wedges
> 12 large button mushrooms, cleaned and stems removed
> 12 cherry tomatoes, washed and stems removed
> 1 tbsp (15 mL) rice vinegar
> 1 tbsp (15 mL) lemon juice
> 1 tsp (5 mL) sesame oil
> 1 tbsp (15 mL) water

Thread veggies on skewers alternately. Combine the vinegar, lemon juice, sesame oil and water in a small bowl. Brush kebobs with vinegar mixture. Preheat grill to medium-high with grill 8 inches (20 cm) from the heat source. Lightly oil barbeque grill and place skewers on it. Cook kebobs until veggies are tender, about 5 minutes per side.

Herbed Baked Potatoes

Herbs are extremely easy to grow, even for apartment dwellers —
just put a few pots on your balcony or windowsill. Snip off a fresh
sprig whenever a recipe calls for it. These potatoes resemble chia
pets (remember those?) when you place the herbs into the slits.

> 6 squares 8-inch x 8-inch (20 cm x 20 cm)
>   aluminum foil
> 6 medium baking potatoes
> 1 bunch fresh rosemary
> 1 bunch fresh thyme
> 1 bunch fresh oregano
> 1/4 cup (50 mL) vegetable stock or water

Wash and scrub the potatoes. Being careful not to cut all of the way
through to the bottom, make slits (about 5 slits per potato) 1/2
inch (1 cm) apart in each potato. Wash the rosemary, thyme and
oregano, and cut into 1-inch (2.5 cm) pieces. Place pieces of each
herb into the slits in the potatoes.

Put each potato onto a piece of foil and brush with stock. Preheat
grill to medium-high with grill 8 inches (20 cm) from the heat
source. Fold the foil tightly around each potato and cook on the
grill, lid closed, for 30 minutes. Turn the potatoes occasionally to
cook evenly.

Flim Flam Fruit Flan

Serves 8

Per serving:
Calories: 192
Fat: 1.3 g

Strawberries symbolize the beginning of summer for many people. Summer always seems far too short, so get outside and enjoy it while you can. If you get a chance, go to a strawberry farm to pick strawberries. Nothing compares to sitting in a strawberry patch in the warm sun, putting more strawberries into you than into the basket.

Crust:
1/2 cup (125 mL) skim milk
1 tsp (5 mL) margarine
1 egg
1 egg white
2/3 cup (150 mL) sugar
1 tsp (5 mL) vanilla extract
1 tsp (5 mL) lemon juice
grated zest of 1 lemon
1 cup (250 mL) all-purpose flour
1 tsp (5 mL) baking powder
pinch of salt

4 cups (1 L) fruit:

It's always best to use what's in season for the freshest taste. For example, you could use straw-berries, peaches, plums, kiwi or mandarin oranges. You could also use one type of fruit only or a combination of 2 or more types.

Glaze:
1/4 cup (50 mL) apricot jam
3 tbsp (50 mL) orange juice
2 tbsp (25 mL) orange liqueur
2 tsp (10 mL) grated orange zest

Preheat oven to 350°F (180°C). Lightly spray a 9- or 10-inch (about 1.5 L) flan pan with non-stick cooking spray and set aside.

Heat the milk in a small saucepan to the scalding point. Add the margarine and stir until it has melted. Set the pan aside to cool slightly. In a medium mixing bowl, combine the egg and egg white, and beat until foamy. Gradually beat in the sugar, vanilla extract, lemon juice and lemon zest.

Combine the flour, baking powder and salt in a small mixing bowl. Stir the dry ingredients into the egg mixture and add the scalded milk. Beat until the mixture is smooth. Pour the mixture into the flan pan. Bake for 20 for 25 minutes. Remove and let cool completely. Arrange your fruit of choice in an attractive pattern over the flan shell.

Whisk together the jam, orange juice, liqueur and orange zest. Spread the glaze over the fruit, covering completely. Refrigerate the flan for 1 hour before serving.

Canadian Coffee

Serve this special drink to your guests after dinner. Ask them to join you on the patio or balcony to watch the sun set on another perfect, Canadian summer day.

> 1 large wedge of lemon
> 1/4 cup (50 mL) sugar, placed on a flat dish
> 6 oz (150 mL) Canadian whisky
> 6 cups (1.5 L) fresh brewed coffee
> 2 tbsp (30 mL) pure maple syrup
> low-fat whipped topping

Run the lemon wedge around the rims of 6 specialty coffee glasses. Dip each rim into the sugar. Pour 1 ounce (30 mL) of whiskey into each glass and top with coffee. Stir 1 teaspoon (5 mL) maple syrup into each glass and top with 1 tablespoon (15 mL) whipped topping. Serve immediately.

For a variation, drizzle the maple syrup over the whipped topping instead of stirring it into the coffee.

Menu 4

How the West Was Won

Okanagan Peach Daiquiris
Carrot-Ginger Vichyssoise
Alberta Peppercorn Steak
Rodeo Rice
Saskatoon Berries with Fromage Blanc

Cocktails

Okanagan Peach Daiquiris

Serves 4

Per serving:
Calories: 180

Fresh peaches from the Okanagan valley, a hint of orange and lime, yum. Get out the blender and whip up this fabulously slushy before-dinner drink for your guests. It's fun to include a special drink as part of your menu, and this one can be easily adapted into a non-alcoholic cocktail for youngsters and those who don't want alcohol. Simply omit the rum and use orange juice concentrate in place of the liqueur.

> 4 cups (1 L) ice cubes
> 8 peach halves, fresh or canned (drained), peeled
> 5 oz (150 mL) white rum
> 3 oz (100 mL) orange-flavored liqueur
> 1/4 cup (50 mL) lime juice
> unpeeled peach wedges for garnish

Blend all ingredients except peach wedges in a blender until smooth. Serve in tall glasses, each garnished with a wedge of unpeeled peach.

Carrot-Ginger Vichyssoise

This soup has an Asian influence so we wanted to include it in our Western menu to honor the Eastern immigrants who have settled in British Columbia. Embracing the differences in culture and cuisine is one of the most wonderful parts of this great country of ours.

1 tsp (5 mL) olive oil
1 clove garlic, minced
1 piece (1-inch/2.5-cm) fresh ginger, sliced
4 medium carrots, peeled and chopped
1 leek (white part only), washed well and sliced
1 potato, peeled and chopped
1 bay leaf
4 cups (1 L) de-fatted chicken stock
salt and pepper to taste
1 cup (250 mL) low-fat milk

Heat the oil in a large saucepan over medium heat. Add the garlic and ginger and sauté for 1 minute. Add the carrots, leek and potato, and sauté for 3 to 4 minutes. Turn the heat to high and add the bay leaf and chicken stock. Bring to a boil, reduce heat and simmer until all vegetables are soft, about 20 minutes.

Remove the soup from the heat and purée in a food processor or blender until smooth. Return the soup to the saucepan and add the salt and pepper to taste. Add the milk, stirring to combine.

At this point, you can refrigerate the soup until serving time or, if you would like to serve the soup hot, you can slowly reheat it over low heat, being careful not to let it boil.

Alberta Peppercorn Steak

Serves 4

Per serving:
Calories: 168
Fat: 6.5 g

Thanks to our friends Margie and Simon in Calgary, you can enjoy what they claim to be their favorite dish. If Grade A Alberta beef isn't available where you live, look for the freshest, leanest, highest-grade beef you can find — pocketbook permitting, of course.

2 small lean, tender steaks (3/4 lb/350 g total weight)
4 tsp (20 mL) black peppercorns
2 tsp (10 mL) olive oil
3 tbsp (50 mL) brandy or Cognac
3 tbsp (50 mL) chicken stock
1 tbsp (15 mL) chopped fresh parsley

Trim the steaks of all visible fat. Put 3 teaspoons (15 mL) of the peppercorns in a resealable plastic bag and crush with a rolling pin or other heavy object. Press crushed peppercorns into both sides of each steak.

Heat the oil in a skillet. Add the steaks and cook over medium-high heat for about 4 minutes per side for medium rare or 7 minutes per side for well done. Remove the steaks from skillet once they have reached the desired doneness and keep warm on a plate in the oven. Add the brandy and chicken stock to skillet over medium heat, stirring to scrape up any browned bits of meat stuck to the skillet. Stir in the remaining teaspoon (5 mL) peppercorns and parsley. Cook for 1 minute.

Slice the steaks thinly across the grain, allowing 1/2 a steak per person. Place the steaks on a serving plate and drizzle the sauce over them.

Serves 4

Per serving:

Calories: 188
Fat: 1.9 g

Rodeo Rice

The Calgary Stampede is considered by many to be the greatest outdoor show on Earth. Cowboys and cowgirls, bucking broncos and the friendliest people you could ever hope to meet all converge here. Alberta also boasts wild rice as part of its agricultural bounty.

> 1 tsp (5 mL) olive oil
> 1/4 cup (50 mL) chopped onion
> 1 cup (250 mL) wild rice
> 1 tbsp (15 mL) chopped fresh parsley
> 1 tbsp (15 mL) snipped fresh chives
> 1 tbsp (15 mL) chopped fresh thyme
> salt and pepper to taste
> 2 1/2 cups (625 mL) water
> 1 red pepper, seeded, cut into 1/4-inch/6 mm-
>   wide strips
> 2 green onions, sliced

Heat the oil in a large saucepan over medium-high heat. Add the onion and sauté until it begins to soften, about 2 minutes. Add the rice and stir to combine with the onion. Add the parsley, chives and thyme as well as the salt, pepper and water. Bring to a boil. Cover and reduce heat. Simmer until all the liquid is absorbed and the rice is tender, about 40 minutes.

Put the red pepper and green onion in a serving bowl. Add the rice and toss to combine. Serve immediately.

Saskatoon Berries with Fromage Blanc

Serves 4

Per serving:

Calories: 103
Fat: 0.4 g

If saskatoon berries are available to you, by all means use the elusive little things. If you can't get ahold of any saskatoon berries, substitute blueberries. Frozen berries also work well in this recipe, but just cut the lemon juice and sugar proportions in half. We serve the berries with a low-fat version of a classic fromage blanc.

> 2 1/2 cups (625 mL) fresh saskatoon berries or
>   blueberries (set aside a few for garnish)
> 3 tbsp (50 mL) lemon juice
> 1 tbsp (15 mL) sugar
> lemon peel curls and mint leaves for garnish
>
> Fromage Blanc:
> 1 cup (250 mL) plain non-fat yogurt
> 1 1/2 cups (375 mL) non-fat cottage cheese

Put the berries in a bowl and toss with the lemon juice and sugar. Cover and refrigerate until the berries have released their juices, about 1 to 2 hours.

Blend the yogurt and cottage cheese in a food processor or blender until smooth and set aside.

Put the berries and juice in a large bowl. With a fork, lightly mash some of the berries. Mix in the fromage blanc. Cover the bowl and refrigerate until well chilled, about 1 hour. Spoon into serving dishes and garnish with a few reserved berries or curls of lemon peel and mint leaves.

Chapter 2

Born in the U.S.A.

New York After-Theater Cocktail Party

Sinless Salmon Dip with Crudités
5th Avenue Shrimp
Soho Sundried Spirals
Cosmopolitan Chicken Spirals
Wild Mushroom Crostini

Pennsylvania-Dutch Sunday Dinner

Creamy Corn Chowder
Salad with Warm Cider Dressing
Pork Tenderloin Stuffed with Apples and Prunes
Sugar Snap Peas and Baby Carrots
Braised Red Cabbage
Smashed Idahos
Ginger Peaches and Cream

Southern Spread

Shrimp and Okra Stew
Creole Rice and White Rice
Carolina Cornmeal Muffins
Hoppin' John Salad
Pineapple Upside-Down Cake

California Chic

Warm Artichoke Dip
Hang Ten Tuna with Mango-Citrus Salsa
City of Angels Pasta
Malibu Meringues

From sea to shining sea, our neighbors to the south have loads of traditional dishes for us to choose from. We chose our favorites and recreated them Wendy and Barb style. That is, we transformed them from dangerously fatty recipes to lean dishes that help make us strong. Going to the theater with some friends? Check out our New York After-Theater Cocktail Party. Fast and easy to prepare before you leave for the theater, fun and effortless when you return. Can you have a martini? Sure. Try to have just one, but don't stress if you have two. There's lots you can do after your guests leave to burn those martini calories away.

Attempting to capture the spirit of the Mid-East, we came up with a Pennsylvania-Dutch Sunday Dinner. You know how much we love our family get-togethers. Creamy Corn Chowder, Pork Tenderloin Stuffed with Apples and Prunes, Braised Red Cabbage and Smashed Idahos. We think this dinner is smashing. And an after-dinner walk with family or friends is a great excuse to spend some quality time with them as well as exercising your body.

Cajun tunes and Cajun spices are on the agenda as we head down the Mississippi to the southern states. Keeping in style with the great southern cooking of seafood and spices, we're giving you Shrimp and Okra Stew, Creole Rice (a staple with most Cajun meals) and Carolina Corn Muffins, amongst other dishes.

How about a little California dreaming? The infamous land of promise, to where starry-eyed people from around the world flock in the hope of being discovered. It seems that the hippest and coolest trends are conceived in the land of the sun. Just some of the dishes we have created in honor of the West Coast are the Warm Artichoke Dip and the grilled Tuna with Mango-Citrus Salsa, as well as City of Angels Pasta. We've even come up with Malibu Meringues. Can't believe it's all low-fat? Well, we guarantee that it is, and delicious on top of that. Move over burgers and fries and make way for a revolution Wendy and Barb style — low-fat, delectable and fun. Remember, you don't have to be the Statue of Liberty to stand tall and proud; you can make every day Independence Day.

Menu 1

New York After-Theater Cocktail Party

Sinless Salmon Dip with Crudités
5th Avenue Shrimp
Soho Sundried Spirals
Cosmopolitan Chicken Spirals
Wild Mushroom Crostini

Wine Suggestions

Champagne or Sparkling Wine

Makes 2 1/2 cups (625 mL)

Per serving: (2 tbsp/30 mL):

**Calories: 51
Fat: 0.8 g**

Sinless Salmon Dip with Crudités

This is an extremely chic dip. All of the vegetables we have suggested here are green, white or a combination of these two colors, and they make an exquisite presentation surrounding the bowl of pale pink dip. Use whichever vegetables you like, but do try the asparagus — it's an unusual addition.

Dip:
1 1/2 cups (375 mL) low- or non-fat sour cream or once-drained Yogo Cheese (see page 24 for recipe)
grated zest of 1 lemon
2 tbsp (25 mL) lemon juice
3 tbsp (50 mL) snipped fresh dill
8 oz (250 g) smoked salmon, finely chopped
fresh dill sprigs for garnish
smoked salmon or salmon caviar for garnish

Mix together the sour cream, lemon zest, lemon juice and dill in a medium-sized bowl. Gently fold in the chopped salmon. Refrigerate the dip in a serving dish until ready to use. Garnish with fresh dill sprigs, a small amount of julienned smoked salmon or a small amount of salmon caviar.

Crudités:
1 lb (500 g) very thin asparagus spears, stem ends trimmed

1/2 lb (250 g) snow peas or sugar snap peas,
    trimmed, strings removed
1 large English cucumber, cut in spears or rounds
1 large daikon (white radish), 1 to 2 inches (2 to 5
    cm) in diameter, peeled and sliced
2 bunches green onions, ends trimmed, green
    tops cut just to even out

Bring a large pot of water to the boil. Add the asparagus and blanch 1 minute. Add the peas and blanch 1 minute more. Drain the vegetables and immediately plunge them into a bowl of ice water. Drain and refrigerate until ready to serve.

Arrange the crudités on a serving platter, with the smoked salmon dip in the middle.

Postcards from the Edge

In the Kitchen

Always store mushrooms in the refrigerator in a paper bag or lightly wrapped in paper towels, never in a plastic bag. Gently wipe mushrooms with a damp cloth or paper towel to clean them. If you wash them in water, they will absorb it like a sponge and become mushy. Yuk.

Serves 20

Per serving:
Calories: 18
Fat: 0.3 g

5th Avenue Shrimp

When it's time to celebrate, splurge with this shrimp appetizer. Elegantly served in endive leaves, it makes a great addition to any cocktail party or buffet.

2 small heads Belgian endive
20 large shrimp, in their shells

Marinade:
1/4 cup (50 mL) lemon juice
1 tbsp (15 mL) soy sauce
2 tsp (10 mL) olive oil
2 tsp (10 mL) grated fresh ginger
2 cloves garlic, finely minced
1/4 cup (50 mL) chopped fresh cilantro or parsley

Trim the ends of endive and separate the leaves. Select 20 of the largest, unblemished leaves. Wash and pat dry. Refrigerate until ready to serve.

Pinch the legs off the shrimp and remove the shells, leaving the tails intact. Wash and pat dry.

Mix together the lemon juice, soy sauce, oil, ginger, garlic and cilantro in a glass dish and add the shrimp. Turn the shrimp to coat. Refrigerate for 1 to 2 hours.

Preheat oven to 375°F (190°C). Bake the shrimp, still in the marinade in the glass dish, uncovered, until the shrimp are pink and just cooked, about 10 minutes. Remove the shrimp from the oven and allow to cool slightly at room temperature.

Arrange the endive leaves on a serving platter. Place 1 shrimp into each endive leaf and serve either warm or cold.

Soho Sundried Spirals

Makes about 36 spirals

Per serving (2 spirals):
Calories: 174
Fat: 4.8 g

Those innocent-looking tidbits at cocktail parties usually add up to a wallop of calories and fat. Well, not at our soirées. Peanuts and cocktail weenies take a walk. We keep it slim and tasty. The sundried tomatoes in this recipe pack a flavor punch, and they look great too.

Sundried Tomato Pesto:
1/2 cup (125 mL) sundried tomatoes (not packed in oil)
1 clove garlic
1 tbsp (15 mL) balsamic vinegar
1 tbsp (15 mL) chopped fresh basil
1 tbsp (15 mL) olive oil
1/4 tsp (1 mL) salt
1/4 tsp (1 mL) pepper

Place the tomatoes in a bowl and add enough warm water to just cover. Let soak for 20 to 30 minutes. Drain and reserve liquid.

Purée the tomatoes, garlic, vinegar, basil, oil, salt and pepper in a blender until the mixture is fairly smooth but still has some texture. If the mixture is too dry, add a little of the tomato liquid while pulsing.

Tortillas:
1/2 cup (125 mL) Yogo Cheese (see page 24 for recipe)
1/2 cup (125 mL) low- or non-fat ricotta cheese
6 12-inch (30-cm) soft flour tortillas

Combine the Yogo Cheese and ricotta in a small bowl.

Spread out 1 tortilla and top with about 3 tablespoons (45 ml) of the cheese mixture, spreading almost to edge of tortilla.

Top with 1 tablespoon (15 mL) of the tomato pesto and spread to a thin, even layer. Roll tightly and wrap with plastic wrap. Repeat procedure with remaining tortillas and refrigerate for 1 hour. (You can also freeze the tortillas if you're preparing them ahead.)

Preheat oven to 350°F (180°C). Remove the tortillas from refrigerator, unwrap and, with a sharp knife, cut each roll into 1 1/2-inch (4-cm) slices. Spray a baking sheet with non-stick cooking spray and place the spirals on tray. Bake until lightly browned and the cheese has melted, about 10 to 15 minutes.

Postcards from the Edge

Just Remember

Through the art of multicultural cooking, we can learn about different peoples and different lands. We hope it will inspire you to go out and learn more about a country that interests you. Maybe it will even persuade you to take a trip there. More importantly, we hope it will teach us to have more tolerance towards people who are different from us. It's the differences that make us all unique and special. It's a big, big world out there, so don't limit yourself.

Cosmopolitan Chicken Spirals

Makes 30 pieces

Per serving (2 pieces):
Calories: 77
Fat: 1.7 g

We've placed the chicken spirals in radicchio leaves for easy eating while you're standing and mingling. You won't be sending that little black dress to the cleaners after this evening.

> 4 large boneless, skinless chicken breasts, halved
> spinach stuffing (recipe follows)
> 1/2 cup (125 mL) all-purpose flour
> salt and pepper to taste
> 1 tbsp (15 mL) olive oil
> 1/4 cup (50 mL) balsamic vinegar
> 3/4 cup (175 mL) de-fatted chicken stock
> 2 small heads radicchio, washed and dried, ends
>   trimmed, leaves separated to make 30 pieces
>
> Stuffing:
> 1/2 package (10 oz/280 g) frozen spinach,
>   thawed, well drained and chopped
> 1 clove garlic, finely minced
> 1/4 cup (50 mL) finely chopped red pepper
> 1/8 tsp (0.5 mL) ground nutmeg
> salt and pepper to taste

Squeeze the spinach between your hands to remove excess moisture. Combine the spinach, garlic, red pepper, nutmeg, salt and pepper in a medium-sized bowl.

Pound each half chicken breast between two sheets of waxed

paper, to 1/4-inch (6-mm) thickness. Top 1 breast with 1 1/2 table-spoons (25 mL) of stuffing, spreading the mixture but not allowing it to touch the edge of the breast. Fold the two thin ends of the breast in 1/2 inch (1 cm), then roll the breast lengthwise, securing with toothpicks. Repeat procedure with remaining breasts.

Put the flour, salt and pepper on a flat plate. Heat the oil in a non-stick skillet over medium heat. Dredge each breast in the flour, shake off excess and place in the skillet. Brown breasts on all sides, turning often, 3 to 5 minutes. Add vinegar to the skillet and cook for 1 minute. Add the stock and bring to a boil. Reduce heat and simmer gently until breasts are cooked through, about 5 minutes.

Transfer the breasts to a cutting board and remove toothpicks. Slice each breast into 1 1/2-inch (4-cm) spirals. Arrange the radic-chio leaves on a platter and place one chicken spiral in each. Spoon a small amount of sauce over each chicken spiral and serve.

Wild Mushroom Crostini

Makes 24
crostini

Per serving
(1 crostini):

Calories: 61
Fat: 1.0 g

There are so many varieties of mushrooms to choose from, each with its own distinctive look and taste. Take a chance and try them all. Go wild for wild mushrooms.

> 1 baguette, sliced on the diagonal into 1/2-inch
>   (1-cm) pieces
> 2 tsp (10 mL) olive oil
> 1 to 2 cloves garlic, peeled
> 1 tbsp (15 mL) de-fatted chicken stock
> 1 shallot, finely minced
> 12 oz (350 g) mixed wild mushrooms (oyster,
>   portobello, cremini), coarsely chopped
> 1/4 cup (5 mL) chopped fresh parsley
> 1 tsp (5 mL) dried thyme
> salt and pepper to taste

Preheat oven to 400°F (200°C). Brush each side of the bread slices lightly with the oil. Place on baking sheet and bake in oven until golden brown, about 4 minutes per side. Remove from oven and rub the garlic clove against one side of each slice. Set aside.

Heat the chicken stock in a large skillet. Add the shallot and cook over medium heat for 1 minute. Add the mushrooms, parsley and thyme and increase the heat to high. Cook for 5 minutes, stirring occasionally, until mushrooms have softened and most of the liquid has evaporated. Season with salt and pepper. Top each bread slice with the mushroom mixture. Serve on a large platter.

Menu 2

Pennsylvania-Dutch Sunday Dinner

Creamy Corn Chowder
Salad with Warm Cider Dressing
Pork Tenderloin Stuffed with Apples and Prunes
Sugar Snap Peas and Baby Carrots
Braised Red Cabbage
Smashed Idahos
Ginger Peaches and Cream

Wine Suggestions

Gallo Sonoma, Cabernet Sauvignon, California

For Beer Lovers

Why not try a cider with our menu?
We recommend
Woodchuck Amber Cider.

Creamy Corn Chowder

Serves 6

Per serving:
Calories: 132
Fat: 2.0 g

Celebrate the fall harvest with our creamy corn chowder. We use evaporated skim milk instead of high-fat cream to make the soup smooth and rich — a great trick for any recipe calling for cream.

> 1/4 cup (50 mL) minced onion
> 2 tsp (10 mL) vegetable oil
> 2 large potatoes, peeled and diced
> 2 1/2 cups (625 mL) water
> 2 cups (500 mL) fresh or frozen corn kernels
> 1 tbsp (15 mL) chopped fresh parsley
> 1/4 tsp (1 mL) dried marjoram
> 1/4 tsp (1 mL) celery seeds
> 2 cups (500 mL) skim milk
> 1/2 cup (125 mL) evaporated skim milk
> salt and pepper to taste
> chopped parsley for garnish

Sauté the onion in oil in a large stockpot over medium heat until it begins to soften, about 5 minutes. Add the potatoes, water, corn, parsley, marjoram and celery seeds; cover and bring to a boil. Turn heat down and simmer until potatoes are tender, about 20 minutes.

Add the skim milk and evaporated skim milk and simmer until thickened, being careful not to boil, about 12 to 15 minutes. Season with salt and pepper and serve garnished with additional chopped parsley.

Serves 6

Per serving:
Calories: 72
Fat: 2.1 g

Salad with Warm Cider Dressing

There are ways of getting around bacon. To get that smoky taste, we've substituted lean smoked ham for bacon in this recipe. The contrast of warm dressing on the cool salad greens is a nice surprise.

> 6 cups (1.5 L) mixed salad greens, including a soft
>   Boston lettuce, washed
> 2 tsp (10 mL) vegetable oil
> 1 thin slice (2 oz/30 g) smoked ham, chopped
>   fine
> 1/2 cup (125 mL) minced onion
> 1 tbsp (15 mL) Dijon mustard
> 1/2 tsp (2 mL) cinnamon
> 3/4 cup (175 mL) apple cider

Tear greens into a large salad bowl.

Heat the oil in skillet over medium heat. Add the ham and onion and sauté until onion has softened, about 3 to 5 minutes. Stir in the mustard and cinnamon. Slowly stir in the cider. Cook for 2 to 3 minutes. Keep warm. Toss the dressing and the greens just before serving.

Pork Tenderloin Stuffed with Apples and Prunes

Serves 6

Per serving:
Calories: 237
Fat: 4.5 g

Pork tenderloin is a very lean cut of pork. Make sure you cook it with some liquid and baste it while it's cooking so it doesn't dry out. Stuffed with prunes and apples, it makes a beautiful presentation when sliced.

> 2 pork tenderloins (1 1/2 to 2 lb/750 g to 1 kg
>   total weight), trimmed of fat
> 3/4 cup (175 mL) apple, cored, peeled and diced
> 3/4 cup (175 mL) pitted prunes, chopped
> 1/4 cup (50 mL) dried bread crumbs
> 2 tbsp (25 mL) finely chopped onion
> 2 tsp (10 mL) finely chopped fresh rosemary
> salt and pepper to taste
> 1 1/2 cups (375 mL) apple juice or apple cider
> 1 tbsp (15 mL) cornstarch

Preheat oven to 400°F (200°C).

Cut a slit lengthwise down one side of each tenderloin to make a pocket, being careful not to cut all the way through the meat. Stop cutting just before each end of the tenderloin.

Mix the apple, prunes, bread crumbs, onion and rosemary in a large bowl. Season with salt and pepper and mix well. Add 1 tablespoon (15 mL) of the apple juice if the mixture is too dry and mix again.

Stuff the mixture into each pocket in the tenderloins and tie securely with kitchen string or use wooden toothpicks to close. Place the tenderloins on a rack in a shallow roasting pan and pour a few tablespoons of the apple juice over them.

Bake until a meat thermometer inserted in the meat registers 160°F (70°C), about 30 minutes. Occasionally pour a little of the apple juice (about 1/3 cup/75 mL total) over tenderloins as they bake.

For sauce: Heat the remaining apple juice, about 1 cup (250 mL), and cornstarch in a small saucepan, whisking constantly. Bring to a boil and stir until slightly thickened, about 1 minute. Pour the sauce over the tenderloins just before serving.

Postcards from the Edge

Living a Healthy Lifestyle

Take time to realistically determine what weight and body shape is right for you. Instead of striving for perfection, work on developing a positive body image which in turn will allow you to focus on your health and how you feel.

That famous southern belle Scarlett said, "As God is my witness, I'll never go hungry again," and neither should you. The worst thing you could possibly do is starve yourself. You need to feed your body properly in order to keep it running like a well-oiled machine. When your body doesn't get enough calories, it prepares itself for a famine by storing fat.

Did you know that the average 130-pound (60-kg) female can burn 264 calories playing recreational football in just one hour? So instead of sitting on the couch being a spectator, get your family or friends out to the park and have a game of America's favorite sport. If football isn't your thing, try soccer or Frisbee — anything to get moving. Doing things with your family or friends will help you feel like you have support and aren't alone in this fight against fat.

Sugar Snap Peas and Baby Carrots

Serves 6

Per serving:
Calories: 74
Fat: 1.6 g

We think sugar snap peas are a delicacy. The pods are so tender, they can be eaten whole. The sweetness of the baby carrots and snap peas together make the addition of fatty sauces and toppings unnecessary for this dish.

> 1 lb (500 g) baby carrots, washed
> 3 cups (750 mL) sugar snap peas, washed, stem
>   ends removed
> 2 tsp (10 mL) soft margarine
> 3 tbsp (50 mL) lemon juice
> salt and pepper to taste

Put carrots in a saucepan and add 1 cup (250 mL) water. Cover and bring to a boil. Cook over medium heat until tender, about 12 minutes. Drain and set aside.

Pull back the strings on the peas to the blossom ends. Put the peas in a saucepan and add 1 cup (250 mL) of water. Cover and bring to the boil. Cook over medium heat for 2 minutes. Drain and set aside.

Melt the margarine in a large skillet. Stir in the lemon juice, salt and pepper. Add the carrots and peas and toss to coat. Serve immediately.

Braised Red Cabbage

Many people aren't big cabbage fans, but maybe that's because they've never tried our slow-braised red cabbage. Cooked gently with red wine, honey and nutmeg, frumpy old cabbage gets a new life. Cabbage is part of the cruciferous family, those vegetables that studies have shown to help fight against cancer. Is that great news or what? Eat your cabbage.

> 1 tsp (5 mL) vegetable oil
> 1 red onion, chopped
> 1 lb (500 g) red cabbage, cored and shredded
> 1/4 cup (50 mL) red wine
> 1/4 cup (50 mL) red wine vinegar
> 1/4 tsp (1 mL) ground nutmeg
> 1 tbsp (15 mL) honey
> salt and pepper to taste
> 1/3 cup (75 mL)chopped fresh parsley

Heat the oil in a large, heavy saucepan over medium heat. Add the onion and sauté for 5 minutes. Add the cabbage, wine, vinegar, nutmeg, honey, salt and pepper to the saucepan. Stir to coat cabbage.

Cover the saucepan and cook for 30 minutes, stirring occasionally and adding a little water if necessary. Toss with parsley just before serving.

Smashed Idahos

Serves 6

Per serving:
Calories: 107
Fat: 0.2 g

Oh, the humble potato. Squished, squashed, smashed — no matter what the form, we love them. They have to be the ultimate comfort food. Try Yukon Gold potatoes; they have a buttery, golden flesh all on their own, so there's no need to add all that fattening stuff.

> 2 lb (1 kg) potatoes, peeled and quartered
> 1 cup (250 mL) buttermilk
> 2 tbsp (25 mL) chopped fresh parsley
> fresh ground pepper to taste

Put potatoes in a large saucepan with enough water to cover them. Bring to a boil and cook until tender, about 15 minutes. Drain and put the saucepan with the potatoes back on the heat for 1 minute to dry the potatoes. Turn off heat.

Heat the buttermilk in a small saucepan until just warm. Mash the potatoes with a potato masher or a fork, adding the buttermilk slowly until you reach the desired consistency. Stir in the parsley and season with pepper.

Serves 6

Per serving:
Calories: 243
Fat: 1.7 g

Ginger Peaches and Cream

Thank goodness some of the large food manufacturers out there have heard our plea for low-fat desserts. The "cream" in this dessert is low-fat ice cream or frozen yogurt, and it actually tastes good. Experiment with different brands. We've gilded the lily here with the addition of Ginger Peaches to create a warm, spicy ending to our harvest dinner.

> 6 fresh peaches
> 1/2 cup (125 mL) sugar
> 2 cups (500 mL) water
> 1 cup (250 mL) dry white wine
> 3 whole cloves
> 1/4 cup (50 mL) candied ginger, chopped
> 1% ice cream or low-fat frozen yogurt

Blanch peaches in a large pot of boiling water for 1 minute. Put in a bowl of cold water, remove the peels, cut in half and remove the stones.

Bring the sugar, water and wine to a boil in a large saucepan. Add the cloves, ginger and peaches. Reduce heat and simmer the peaches for 15 to 20 minutes. Allow peaches to cool in the wine mixture. Served either warm or cold over 1% ice cream or low-fat frozen yogurt.

Menu 3

Southern Spread

Shrimp and Okra Stew
Creole Rice and White Rice
Carolina Cornmeal Muffins
Hoppin' John Salad
Pineapple Upside-Down Cake

Wine Suggestions

Turning Leaf, Chardonnay, California

Shrimp and Okra Stew

Cajuns, Creoles, African-Americans and Native Indians all stake claims in countless versions of gumbos. There are Cajun, country and urbanized versions from New Orleans, Charleston and Savannah. Although the ingredients may differ slightly, as do the thickening agents, the stew remains a scrumptious one-pot meal that is easy enough for a family dinner but refined enough for entertaining. Our version uses okra, a natural thickener for the stew, along with cornstarch in place of the traditional roux (butter and flour). It all adds up to a spicy, skinny version of a Deep South classic.

2 tbsp (25 mL) vegetable stock
1 green pepper, seeded and cut in large dice
1 red pepper, seeded and cut in large dice
1 stalk celery, sliced
6 green onions, sliced
2 cloves garlic, minced
3 cups (750 mL) de-fatted chicken stock
1 bay leaf
2 tsp (10 mL) dried thyme
1 1/2 tsp (7 mL) hot pepper sauce
2 packages (10 oz/280 g each) frozen sliced okra
2 lb (1 kg) medium shrimp, shelled and deveined
2 1/2 cups (625 mL) frozen corn
2 tsp (10 mL) cornstarch
1 tbsp (15 mL) water
salt and pepper to taste

Heat the vegetable stock in a large stockpot over medium heat. Add the peppers, celery, onions and garlic. Sauté until vegetables begin to soften, about 5 minutes. Add the chicken stock, bay leaf, thyme and hot pepper sauce, stirring to combine. Bring to a boil. Add the okra, reduce heat to a simmer, cover and cook for 10 minutes. Add the corn and cook about 3 minutes. Turn heat back to high and bring the stew to a boil.

Mix together the cornstarch and water. Add shrimp and corn-starch-and-water mixture at same time and cook, stirring constantly until liquid has thickened slightly and shrimp are just pink. Season with salt and pepper. Spoon rice (recipe follows) into individual-sized serving bowls and ladle the stew over the top.

Note: Shrimp can be costly, so you may want to cut the quantity called for in half. If you do, simply halve the shrimp you use lengthwise. The shrimp will still have their beautiful curved shape so the overall presentation of the stew will be the same, but you've cut down on cost, calories and fat.

Serves 8

Per serving:
Calories: 152
Fat: 0.1 g

Creole Rice

This spicy rice dish makes a great vegetarian meal when served with the Hoppin' John Salad. We also offer a white rice recipe that pairs well with the spicy shrimp stew.

>4 cups (1 L) de-fatted chicken stock
>3 green onions, sliced
>1 red pepper, seeded and minced
>1/4 tsp (1 mL) cayenne
>2 cups (500 mL) long-grain white rice

Preheat oven to 375°F (190°C).

Heat the stock to boiling in a saucepan over medium heat. Put onions, red pepper, cayenne and rice in a large casserole dish. Pour in stock and stir to combine. Bake, covered, until tender and all liquid is absorbed, about 40 to 45 minutes. Turn oven off and leave the rice in oven until ready to serve.

White Rice

◎ ◎ ◎ ◎

Serves 8

Per serving:
Calories: 123
Fat: 0 g

If you prefer, you can substitute plain white rice for the Creole rice in this menu. It compliments the spicy shrimp stew by cooling the palate and adding texture as a side dish. If you've ever had trouble making tender, fluffy rice, give this method a try. It comes out perfect every time.

> 4 cups (1 L) water
> 1/2 tsp (2 mL) salt
> 2 cups (500 mL) long-grain white rice

Put the water and salt in a large pot, cover tightly and bring to a boil. Add the rice and stir quickly to separate the grains. Lower the heat so that the rice is barely simmering. Cook, covered, for 15 minutes. Turn off the heat and let sit, covered tightly, for 15 minutes. Fluff the rice with a fork before serving.

Postcards from the Edge

Exercise Tip

Exercise to music. Not only does music lower your perception of fatigue but the beat may have you moving at a higher intensity.

Serves 12

Per serving:

Calories: 130
Fat: 3.0 g

Carolina Cornmeal Muffins

Cornmeal has been a staple in American diets since the Native peoples first introduced it to the settlers. In the South, grits is a popular dish. It is similar to cream of wheat or porridge and is served either for breakfast or at other meals, where it is topped with gravy. Our muffins are a great accompaniment to the Hoppin' John Salad or for sopping up all the great juices in our spicy Shrimp and Okra Stew.

> 1 cup (250 mL) all-purpose flour
> 1 cup (250 mL) yellow cornmeal
> 3 tbsp (50 mL) sugar
> 1 tbsp (15 mL) baking powder
> 1/4 tsp (1 mL) salt
> 1 cup (250 mL) buttermilk
> 2 egg whites
> 2 tbsp (25 mL) canola oil

Preheat oven to 400°F (200°C). Spray twelve 2 1/2-inch (100 mL) muffin cups with non-stick cooking spray and set aside.

Stir together the flour, cornmeal, sugar, baking powder and salt in a large bowl. In a separate bowl, beat the buttermilk, egg whites and oil. Pour the liquid ingredients into the dry and mix until just incorporated.

Pour the batter into the muffin cups, filling each 3/4 full. Bake until a toothpick inserted in center comes out clean, about 15 minutes.

Hoppin' John Salad

Serves 8

Per serving:
Calories: 179
Fat: 2.1 g

Hoppin' John Salad is traditionally eaten in the South on New Year's Eve to bring good luck to the household in the coming year. Our version omits the rice to make the dish more salad-like.

> 2 cups (500 mL) black-eyed peas, cooked and drained, reserving 3 tbsp (50 mL) of cooking liquid
> 1/2 cup (125 mL) chopped red onion
> 1/4 cup (50 mL) chopped celery
> 1/2 small head romaine lettuce, washed and torn into bite-sized pieces
> 1/2 cup (125 mL) balsamic vinegar
> 2 cloves garlic, minced
> 1 tbsp (15 mL) Dijon mustard
> 1 tbsp (15 mL) olive oil
> 1/2 cup (125 mL) chopped fresh chervil, parsley or chives, or a combination
> salt and pepper to taste

Toss together the peas, onion, celery and lettuce in a large bowl. In a small bowl, whisk together the vinegar, garlic, mustard, oil and reserved cooking liquid. Pour the vinegar dressing over the vegetables, tossing to coat.

Gently toss in the herbs and season with salt and pepper just before serving. This salad is best served at room temperature.

Serves 8

Per serving:

Calories: 230
Fat: 1.8 g

Pineapple Upside-Down Cake

Baking this cake in a cast-iron skillet the traditional way is what makes it so unusual. African and Caribbean influences show themselves in many aspects of southern cooking. The use of pineapple in this dessert is one of those influences.

> 5 slices (3/4 inch/1.5 cm thick) fresh or canned
>   pineapple, juice reserved
> 1/2 cup (125 mL) packed brown sugar
> 9 pecan halves
> 2 egg whites
> 1 large egg, separated
> 1/2 cup (125 mL) granulated sugar
> 1 tsp (5 mL) rum flavoring or vanilla extract
> 3/4 cup (175 mL) all-purpose flour
> 1/2 tsp (2 mL) baking powder
> 1/4 tsp (1 mL) salt

Preheat oven to 350°F (180°C). Lightly spray a 10-inch (25 cm) cast-iron skillet or 10-inch (2 L) cake pan with non-stick cooking spray and set aside.

Cut 4 of the pineapple slices in half, and leave 1 slice whole. Spoon 2 tablespoons (25 mL) of the reserved pineapple juice and the brown sugar into the bottom of the skillet or cake pan, spreading evenly. Put the whole pineapple slice in the middle of the skillet or cake pan and arrange the half slices around it, lightly pressing them into the sugar. Place the pecans into the spaces between the pineapple slices.

Beat the egg whites in a large bowl until stiff. In a second bowl, beat the egg yolk, granulated sugar, 1/4 cup (50 mL) of the reserved pineapple juice and the rum flavoring. Mix together the flour, baking powder and salt and add it to the egg yolk mixture, stirring to combine. Gently fold in the egg whites.

Pour the batter over the pineapple slices and bake for 30 to 35 minutes. Invert at once onto serving plate; leave pan over cake a few minutes. Cut into wedges and serve warm.

Postcards from the Edge

Entertaining

Celebrate American holidays with a dinner party. Since the dates of these holidays change each year (except for Independence Day — we all know when that is), check your calendar; we've given you the months to get you started.

Martin Luther King Day: January
Lincoln's Birthday: February
President's Day: February
Memorial Day: May
Independence Day: July 4
Columbus Day: October
Thanksgiving Day: November

Menu 4

California Chic

Warm Artichoke Dip
Hang Ten Tuna with Mango-Citrus Salsa
City of Angels Pasta
Malibu Meringues

Wine Suggestions

Beringer Proprietor Napa Chardonnay, California

Warm Artichoke Dip

Serves 2

Per serving:
Calories: 101
Fat: 1.8 g

California is one of the main producers of artichokes. Artichokes are believed to be an aphrodisiac, so we have included them here in our chic dinner for two. This warm dip can be served with raw veggies, crackers, low-fat tortilla chips or slices of fresh baguette. This recipe can easily be doubled or tripled.

> 2 tbsp (25 mL) reduced-fat cheese
> 2 tbsp (25 mL) non-fat yogurt or non-fat sour cream
> 2 tbsp (25 mL) reduced-fat mayonnaise
> 1 green onion, trimmed and sliced
> 1 small jar (6-oz/170 g) water-packed artichoke
>   hearts, drained and coarsely chopped

Mix all ingredients together in a small casserole dish. Cover dish and bake at 325°F (160°C) until hot, about 10 to 15 minutes.

Serves 2

Per serving:
Calories: 245
Fat: 3.8 g

Hang Ten Tuna with Mango-Citrus Salsa

Catch a wave with our grilled tuna. Tuna is a mild, firm-fleshed fish, and it is important not to overcook it, so keep your eye on the grill. The fruit salsa is a nice contrast in both taste and texture.

> **2 tuna steaks, about 5 oz (150 g) each**
> **1 tsp (5 mL) vegetable oil**

Brush the tuna steaks on both sides with the oil. Preheat barbeque to medium-high heat with the grill 8 inches (20 cm) from the heat source. Grill the tuna for 4 minutes per side. Fish should be barely opaque in center when done. Remove from grill and keep warm.

> **Mango-Citrus Salsa:**
> **1 orange**
> **1/2 mango**
> **1/2 jalapeño pepper, seeded and finely minced**
>   **(wear gloves for this)**
> **1 clove garlic, finely minced**
> **1 tbsp (15 mL) orange juice concentrate**
> **2 tbsp (25 mL) chopped fresh cilantro**

Remove the skin and pith from orange with a sharp knife. Holding an orange section over a small bowl, cut down either side of membranes, letting the segment drop into the bowl. Repeat with the remaining segments. Using your hands, squeeze the juice from leftover membranes into the bowl.

Cut the mango in half lengthwise, avoiding the pit. Peel and dice the mango flesh and add to the orange segments. Stir in the jalapeño, garlic, orange juice concentrate and cilantro. Refrigerate until ready to use.

Serve tuna steaks topped with salsa.

Postcards from the Edge

Just Remember

Winners never quit and quitters never win.
— *Vince Lombardi*

We can all be winners in the low-fat game.

Serves 2

Per serving:
Calories: 240
Fat: 3.0 g

City of Angels Pasta

Angel hair pasta cooks so quickly that this dish would make a great dinner on its own those nights that you're in a hurry. However, since this menu is suggested as a romantic dinner for two, take it slow. How about a stroll on the beach with your sweetie to watch the sunset before serving dinner outside under the stars?

1/4 lb (125 g) fresh asparagus, cut in 1-inch pieces
2 tsp (10 mL) olive oil
1/4 lb (125 g) mushrooms, cleaned and sliced
grated zest of 1/2 a lemon
2 tbsp (25 mL) chopped fresh basil
salt and pepper to taste
1 tbsp (15 mL) all-purpose flour
1/4 cup (50 mL) de-fatted chicken stock
1/4 cup (50 mL) lemon juice
1/4 lb (125 g) angel hair pasta (capellini)
chopped basil for garnish

Bring 2 cups (500 mL) water to a boil in a saucepan. Blanch the asparagus in the water for 1 minute. Drain, rinse under cold water and set aside.

Place a large pot of water on the stove to boil for the pasta.

Meanwhile, heat the oil in a skillet over high heat. Add the mushrooms and sauté for 1 minute. Turn the heat down to medium and sauté until mushrooms begin to release their juices, about 1 minute. Continue to cook for 1 more minute.

Add the asparagus, lemon zest, 2 tablespoons (25 mL) basil and the salt and pepper. Cook, stirring constantly, for 4 minutes.

Sprinkle the flour over the vegetables, stirring well. Add the stock and lemon juice, bring to a boil and simmer for 2 to 3 minutes. Cover, remove from heat and set aside until pasta is ready.

Add the pasta to the boiling water, watching it carefully, as angel hair pasta cooks very quickly. Test a strand after it has cooked for 5 minutes. Drain well and return to the pot. Add the asparagus sauce and toss well. Serve immediately, garnished with chopped basil.

Malibu Meringues

The secret to making great meringues is to have very clean and dry beaters and bowl. This will seem like a decadent dessert with the silky yogurt and hint of amaretto, but it comes in far under 1 g of fat per serving.

Meringues:
2 large egg whites, at room temperature
1/4 tsp (1 mL) salt
1/4 tsp (1 mL) cream of tartar
1/2 cup (125 mL) granulated sugar
1/2 tsp (2 mL) almond or vanilla extract

Preheat oven to 250°F (120°C). Line a baking sheet with parchment paper and set aside.

Beat the egg whites, salt and cream of tartar in a small bowl until foamy. Gradually beat in the sugar until stiff peaks form. Beat in the almond extract.

Make 6 mounds of the egg white mixture on the baking sheet, leaving space between each. With a spoon, spread each mound into a 3-inch circle, making a well in the center of each. Bake for 45 minutes. Turn oven off and leave in oven for 1 1/2 hours. Don't open the oven door.

Remove the meringues from oven and transfer to a rack to cool. Since you will be using only 2 meringue shells for this recipe, reserve extras for later use. Store in an air-tight container for up to 1 week, or wrap well and freeze.

Filling:

1/2 cup (125 mL) low-fat vanilla yogurt, drained
    in a coffee-filter-lined sieve overnight, or 1/2 cup
    drained plain yogurt flavored with 1 tsp (5 mL)
    amaretto or almond extract.
2 tbsp (25 mL) confectioners' sugar
3/4 cup fresh fruit

Combine the yogurt with the sugar. Spoon the yogurt mixture into
the meringue cups. Top with fresh fruit of your choice. Berries,
especially raspberries, work very well in this dessert.

Chapter 3

Goin' South

Caribbean Dreams

Rum Runners Punch
Sunshine Shrimp and Pineapple Salad
Jerk Chicken with Star Fruit Salsa
Calabaza with Rice and Kale
Calypso Carrot Cake

South American Salsa Spread

Scallop or Mushroom Ceviche
Brazilian Black Bean Salad
Ropa Vieja
Cumin-Scented Rice
Marinated Green Beans
Quinoa Pudding with Tropical Fruit Salad

Freedom from everyday stresses is what attracts most of us to a Caribbean getaway. Home of the Cayman Islands, the Windward Islands, the Grenadines and so many more islands, the Caribbean has been dubbed the "eighth continent" of the world. Whether you choose to envision scuba diving in pristine blue waters, walking the white and black beaches found in the Dominican Republic or simply lounging poolside with a "kill devil" (an old name for rum), we think everyone would like to indulge in a taste of the Caribbean in some way.

It's impossible to capture all of the unique dishes each island is famous for, so we decided to offer you a selection of those dishes that can be easily made using low-fat ingredients. Saluting the soul-warming sun and abundance of fresh fruits available, we've created a Sunshine Shrimp and Pineapple Salad. It's guaranteed to set you sailing the crystal-clear waters, if only in spirit.

Spicy music and spicier foods are just some of the things this eighth continent of the world can brag about. Jerk Chicken with Star Fruit Salsa, and Calabaza with Rice and Kale make us want to get up and move to the Calypso beat.

From the most southern island in the Caribbean, Trinidad, we easily travel into South America. Everybody salsa! Whether you envision the forgotten city of Machu Picchu in Peru, the year-round racetracks of Buenos Aires or the depths of the Amazon, South America offers something for everyone. Likewise, even the pickiest eaters will find something in our South American Salsa Spread that will please them. Ceviche with Scallops or Mushrooms, Brazilian Black Bean Salad and Ropa Vieja are definite crowd pleasers. Your guests might even pipe out, "Muchas Gracias. Mas! Mas!" ("Thank you very much. More! More!")

It wouldn't be a traditional South American experience if the tango wasn't performed at some point during the evening. If you're anything like us, you love to dance and don't have to be asked twice. Why not incorporate these recipes into a romantic evening for two? Crank the heat up with the tango and relax later with traditional panpipe music. Trust us, it definitely sets the mood for a number of things.

Menu 1

Caribbean Dreams

Rum Runners Punch
Sunshine Shrimp and Pineapple Salad
Jerk Chicken with Star Fruit Salsa
Calabaza with Rice and Kale
Calypso Carrot Cake

Cocktails

Rum Runners Punch

What could be more appropriate for our Caribbean menu than rum punch? Can't you just hear the steel-drum band playing and feel the warm island breeze through your hair? Exotic fruit juices and spicy dark rum mix together to make the perfect opening to this tropical dinner.

6 ounces (175 mL) dark rum
1 1/2 cups (375 mL) pineapple juice
1 1/2 cups (375 mL) orange juice
1/2 cup (125 mL) lemon juice
2 tsp (10 mL) Angostura bitters
lime wedges for garnish

Combine all ingredients in a large punch bowl. Pour punch into tall glasses filled with ice and garnish each with a wedge of lime.

6 servings

Per serving:
Calories: 244
Fat: 2.6 g

Sunshine Shrimp and Pineapple Salad

This salad is definitely a palate pleaser. The sweet-tart pineapple paired with shrimp in a creamy but definitely low-fat dressing is a combination made in heaven. A hint of curry adds that island flair.

> 1/2 cup (125 mL) white wine
> 1 1/4 lb (625 g) medium shrimp, shelled and deveined
> 1 small head leaf lettuce
> 1 medium pineapple, trimmed, cored and cut into 3/4-inch (1.5 cm) slices, or 14-oz (398 mL) can sliced pineapple, drained
> 1 medium green pepper, seeded and chopped
> 4 large green onions, sliced
> 3 large stalks celery, sliced
> 3/4 cup (175 mL) plain non-fat yogurt
> 1/4 tsp (1 mL) curry powder
> 2 tbsp (25 mL) pineapple juice
> lemon wedges for garnish

Bring the wine to a simmer in a small skillet over medium heat. Add the shrimp and poach until opaque, about 3 to 5 minutes. Remove the shrimp with a slotted spoon and put in a small bowl. Chill in the refrigerator.

Increase heat under the wine to high and boil the wine for about 5 minutes to reduce to half. Remove the skillet from heat and allow the wine to cool.

Meanwhile, wash the lettuce and pat dry with paper towel. Line 6 salad plates with lettuce leaves and top each with 1 slice of the pineapple.

In a medium-sized bowl, combine the wine, green pepper, green onions, celery, yogurt, curry powder and pineapple juice. Add the shrimp to the dressing mixture and toss lightly. Scoop the shrimp mixture onto the pineapple and lettuce and garnish with lemon wedges.

Postcards from the Edge

In the Kitchen

Cilantro, also called coriander, is a leafy green herb with a slightly lemon taste. It is commonly used in a variety of ethnic cuisines. Store it wrapped in damp paper towel, inside a plastic bag. It will keep fresh in the refrigerator for up to week.

Kale is a member of the cabbage family. It is most commonly used as a garnish but makes an interesting change from spinach in many green side dishes.

Quinoa (pronounced *keen-o-wa*) is a small, pale grain with a wonderful, earthy taste. It is rich in nutrients and readily available in most grocery stores. Easy to cook, it can be served plain as a side dish instead of rice or pasta or turned into a fabulous dessert, as we have done.

Jerk Chicken with Star Fruit Salsa

This is a spicy, authentic Caribbean recipe. We've suggested using one Scotch bonnet or habeñero pepper, but feel free to substitute milder peppers or turn up the heat by adding more if you're a brave soul. The fruit salsa helps to tame the fire and creates a nice texture combination. Star fruit or carambola is a unique fruit that, when sliced, looks like a star, which is what you'll be when you serve this hot little number.

> 1 onion
> 1 Scotch bonnet pepper, seeds removed
> 1 clove garlic
> 1 tbsp (15 mL) brown sugar
> 1 tsp (5 mL) ground allspice
> 1/2 tsp (2 mL) salt
> 1 tsp (5 mL) black pepper
> 1/2 tsp (2 mL) ground nutmeg
> 1/2 tsp (2 mL) cinnamon
> 2 tbsp (25 mL) lime juice
> 1 tbsp (15 mL) water
> 2 tsp (10 mL) vegetable oil
> 4 chicken breasts, bone in, skinless

Chop vegetables in a food processor or blender. Add all other ingredients except the chicken and combine. Pulse on and off to combine marinade. Put the chicken in a glass casserole dish and cover with marinade. Refrigerate for 3 hours or overnight.

Preheat oven to 350°F (180°C). Put the chicken on a rack in a baking pan and bake for about 45 minutes. Brown the chicken under the broiler for about 2 minutes per side for a lovely crispy coating.

Star Fruit Salsa

Makes 2 1/2 cups (625 mL)

Per serving (1/3 cup/ 75 mL):

Calories: 54
Fat: 0 g

Here's that fruit salsa we were telling you about. A perfect accompaniment to the Jerk Chicken.

> 2 star fruit (carambola), thinly sliced
> 1 medium red onion, diced
> 1 red pepper, seeded and diced
> 1/4 cup (50 mL) lime juice
> 2 tbsp (25 mL) honey
> 1/4 cup (50 mL) chopped fresh mint

Combine all ingredients in a medium-sized bowl, tossing together gently. Refrigerate for 1 hour. Spoon salsa over the chicken and serve.

Serves 6

Per serving:
Calories: 221
Fat: 2.1 g

Calabaza with Rice and Kale

Calabaza is a pumpkin grown throughout the Caribbean islands. It is a green and white squash with pale orange flesh and is milder in flavor than jack-o'-lantern pumpkins. Here it is combined with fragrant island spices and kale, a slightly bitter but succulent green.

2 tsp (10 mL) vegetable oil
1 large onion, diced
2 cups (500 mL) diced calabaza or butternut squash
1 Scotch bonnet pepper, seeds removed, minced (wear gloves!)
2 cloves garlic, minced
1 tbsp (15 mL) fresh ginger, minced
1 tsp (5 mL) cumin
1/2 tsp (2 mL) ground cloves
1/2 tsp (2 mL) ground allspice
salt and black pepper to taste
4 cups (1 L) water
2 cups (500 mL) rice
2 cups (500 mL) kale or spinach, washed well and chopped

Sauté the onion, calabaza, Scotch bonnet pepper, garlic and ginger in the oil in a large pot over medium heat until vegetables are soft, about 10 minutes. Add the cloves, allspice, cumin, salt and black pepper and sauté for 2 minutes. Add the water, rice and kale, cover pot and simmer over medium heat for 30 minutes.

Serves 15

Per serving:
Calories: 235
Fat: 3.9 g

Calypso Carrot Cake

Carrot cake is so popular in the Caribbean that a well-known island airline serves it after all passenger meals. Our version, while still flavored with rum and pineapple, and with a gooey icing, is so low in fat, you'll be able to do the limbo after dinner.

2 1/2 cups (625 mL) all-purpose flour
1 1/4 cups (300 mL) brown sugar
2 tsp (10 mL) baking soda
2 tsp (10 mL) ground cinnamon
3/4 cup (175 mL) plus 2 tbsp (25 mL) apple juice
4 egg whites
1 tsp (5 mL) vanilla extract
1 tsp (5 mL) rum flavoring
2 cups (500 mL) grated carrots
1 cup (250 mL) canned, crushed pineapple, drained
1/3 cup (75 mL) raisins

Icing:
1 1/2 cups (375 mL) light cream cheese
1/2 cup (125 mL) confectioners' sugar
1 tsp (5 mL) rum flavoring

Preheat oven to 325°F (160°C). Coat a 9x13-inch (3.5 L) baking pan with non-stick cooking spray.

To make the cake, combine the flour, brown sugar, baking soda and cinnamon in a large bowl, mixing well. Add the apple juice, egg whites, vanilla extract and rum flavoring and stir to combine. Stir in the carrots, pineapple and raisins.

Spread the cake batter evenly in the pan and bake for 30 to 35 minutes. Cool completely in pan on wire rack.

To make the icing, combine the cream cheese, confectioners' sugar and rum flavoring, beating until smooth. Spread the icing over the cooled cake and cut into squares.

This page, clockwise from top:
Smashed Idahos (p. 59)
Salad with Warm Cider Dressing (p. 54)
Ginger Peaches and Cream (p. 60)
Braised Red Cabbage (p. 58)
Sugar Snap Peas and Baby Carrots (p. 57)
Creamy Corn Chowder (p. 53)

Overleaf, clockwise from top:
Calabaza with Rice and Kale (p. 86)
Jerk Chicken (p. 84)
Star Fruit Salsa (p. 85)
Sunshine Shrimp and Pineapple Salad (p. 82)
Calypso Carrot Cake (p. 87)
Rum Runners Punch (p. 81)

Menu 2

South American Salsa Spread

Scallop or Mushroom Ceviche
Brazilian Black Bean Salad
Ropa Vieja
Cumin-Scented Rice
Marinated Green Beans
Quinoa Pudding with Tropical Fruit Salad

Wine Suggestions

Santa Carolina, Cabernet Sauvignon Reserve, Chile

Serves 8

Per serving:
Calories: 147
Fat: 2.2 g

Scallop or Mushroom Ceviche

Ceviche is a method of cooking seafood with citrus juice. When the seafood is marinated in the juice, the flesh changes in composition, becoming opaque and firm, just as it would if you heated it. You must use the freshest seafood for this recipe. However, if the thought of eating seafood that hasn't been cooked with heat doesn't turn you on, simply substitute tiny, whole, button mushrooms for the scallops.

> 1 cup (250 mL) lemon juice
> 1 jalapeño pepper, seeded and finely minced
>   (remember to wear gloves!)
> 1 tsp (5 mL) salt
> 2 lb (1 kg) bay scallops, washed well under cold
>   running water, drained
> 1 red bell pepper, seeded and finely diced
> 4 green onions, thinly sliced
> 2 tsp (10mL) olive oil
> 2 tbsp (25 mL) chopped fresh parsley
> 8 large lettuce leaves, washed and set aside

Combine the lemon juice, jalapeño and salt in a glass bowl. Add the scallops and stir to combine. Cover the bowl with plastic wrap and marinate in the refrigerator for 3 to 4 hours.

Add the red pepper, green onions, oil and parsley to the scallops. Toss and serve on lettuce-lined serving plates.

Brazilian Black Bean Salad

Serves 8

Per serving:
Calories: 223
Fat: 2.1 g

Black beans are a staple of South American diets. Whether cooked in a deliciously thick soup or served with rice, they are a nutritious and economical addition to your menu. When beans are combined with rice or other grains, a complete protein is created — good news if you're pursuing a vegetarian lifestyle. Even if you're not ready to give up meat altogether, eating vegetarian once a week is a healthy alternative to the usual meat-heavy weeknight dinners.

> 4 cups (1 L) cooked black beans, or two cans
>   (19 oz/540 mL) black beans, rinsed and drained
> 1 red onion, finely chopped
> 1 red pepper, seeded and diced
> 1 yellow pepper, seeded and diced
> 1 medium cucumber, peeled, seeded and chopped
> 2 large tomatoes, seeded and chopped
> 1/2 cup (125 mL) chopped fresh parsley
> 1/4 cup (50 mL) chopped fresh cilantro
> 8 large lettuce leaves, red or green leaf, washed
>   and set aside

Dressing:
1/3 cup (75 mL) lemon juice
1 tbsp (15 mL) olive oil
1 tbsp (15 mL) Dijon mustard
1 tsp (5 mL) ground cumin
few drops hot pepper sauce
salt and pepper to taste

Mix the beans and vegetables in a large bowl. In a smaller bowl, whisk together dressing ingredients. Pour the dressing over the beans and toss gently to combine. Cover the bowl and refrigerate for 1 hour before serving.

When ready to serve, line 8 serving plates each with a large leaf of lettuce and top with the bean salad.

Postcards from the Edge

Entertaining

To throw off winters chills, throw a Latin-style party for your friends in mid-January. Find some hot Latin music, maybe even a fake palm tree or two and prepare one of our south-of-the-border menus. If you can get everybody up to merengue and lambada, you can work off calories as well as those winter blues.

Ropa Vieja

Serves 8

Per serving:
Calories: 203
Fat: 6.9 g

"Ropa Vieja" means old clothes or old rags. The name (we hope) refers to how the meat becomes so tender as it cooks that it falls apart in shreds. This is a good recipe for a lean but not-so-tender cut of meat, such as flank steak. You *can* eat beef on a low-fat diet, just remember to buy lean cuts and keep your portion size to between 3 and 5 ounces (90 and 150 g).

> 2-lb (1 kg) flank steak, well trimmed, cut in half
> 4 quarts (4 L) water
> 6 cloves garlic, unpeeled
> 1 large onion, quartered
> 1 large carrot, peeled, cut in large chunks
> 2 stalks celery with leaves, coarsely chopped
> 2 dried red chilies
> 1 tsp (5 mL) black peppercorns
> 1 tsp (5 mL) salt
> chopped fresh parsley for garnish

Put the steak in the bottom of a large stockpot. Pour the water over it and add the remaining ingredients except the parsley. Bring to a boil and cook for 10 minutes. Lower heat, cover and simmer over low heat for 1 1/2 to 2 hours.

Remove the stockpot from heat and allow the meat to cool in its stock. Remove the meat from the stock, placing on a cutting board. Discard the stock or de-fat for use in another recipe (you can freeze it if you like). Using a fork or your fingers, shred the meat and set aside.

Sauce:

2 tsp (10 mL) olive oil
1 large onion, halved and thinly sliced
1 green pepper, seeded and thinly sliced
2 cloves garlic, finely minced
2 cups (500 mL) drained and chopped whole
  tomatoes
1/2 cup (125 mL) red wine
salt and pepper to taste

In a large skillet, heat the oil over medium-low heat. Add the onion, green pepper and garlic and sauté until softened, about 5 minutes. Add the tomatoes and wine and increase heat to medium. Cook, uncovered, for 10 to 15 minutes. Stir in the shredded beef and the salt and black pepper. Cook for an additional 20 to 30 minutes over low heat. Transfer to a serving dish and garnish with parsley.

Postcards from the Edge

Just Remember

You have to expect things of yourself before you can do them.
— Michael Jordan

Waiting around for changes to magically occur does you no good. There are no fairy godmothers that we know of. Nobody can change your life but you.

Cumin-Scented Rice

Serves 6

Per serving:
Calories: 187
Fat: 1.5 g

The secret to this rice dish is sautéing the cumin seeds before the liquid is added. The seeds release their natural oils and fill the air with a subtle aroma when they hit the hot skillet. We suggest you use long-grain white rice in this recipe because we find it cooks up light and fluffy, but you could also use brown rice. If you do, be sure to adjust the amount of liquid and cooking time according to the package directions.

> 2 tsp (10 mL) olive oil
> 2 cups (500 mL) long-grain white rice, rinsed and
>   drained
> 1 tsp (5 mL) cumin seeds
> 1 small onion, finely diced
> 1 clove garlic, minced
> salt and pepper to taste
> 2 cups (500 mL) de-fatted chicken stock
> 2 cups (500 mL) water

Heat the oil in a skillet over high heat. Add well-drained rice and sauté, stirring constantly for 3 to 5 minutes. Reduce heat to medium and add the cumin seeds, onion and garlic. Cook for 3 minutes. Season with salt and pepper. Add the stock and water. Bring to a boil over high heat, stir, reduce heat to a simmer and cover. Simmer until rice is tender and all liquid has been absorbed, about 15 minutes.

Serve alongside the Ropa Vieja (recipe on page 93).

Marinated Green Beans

This piquant side dish has a combination of hot, sweet and sour that will add interest to any meal. Adjust the amount of red pepper flakes to your own taste. You know us. We like things hot and spicy, so even poor old green beans don't stand a chance of being boring around us.

> 1 1/2 lb (750 g) fresh green beans, ends trimmed
> 1 small onion, thinly sliced into rings
> 1/3 cup (75 mL) red wine vinegar
> 2 tbsp (25 mL) lemon juice
> 2 tsp (10 mL) olive oil
> 1 clove garlic, minced
> 1 tbsp (15 mL) sugar
> 2 tbsp (25 mL) chopped fresh parsley
> 1/4 tsp (1 mL) red pepper flakes
> 1 tsp (5 mL) salt
> fresh ground black pepper

Bring a pot of water to a boil. Add the beans and cook until just barely tender, about 8 minutes. Drain the beans and put them in a large bowl. Add the remaining ingredients and toss well to combine. Marinate for 1 hour at room temperature, or in the refrigerator if you prefer to serve the dish cold.

Quinoa Pudding

If any of you have read our first book, you'll know that couscous pudding was a staple comfort-food for us. It kept us going on our journey to a low-fat lifestyle. Well, here's a new twist on an old grain. Quinoa has been a staple as far back as the time of the Inca. We hope this becomes a favorite dessert of yours, too.

> 1 1/2 cups (375 mL) raw quinoa
> 2 1/2 cups (625 mL) 1% milk
> 3/4 cup (175 mL) sugar
> 1/4 tsp (1 mL) salt
> 1/2 tsp (2 mL) cinnamon
> 1/8 tsp (0.5 mL) ground cloves
> 1/2 tsp (2 mL) vanilla extract
> 1/4 cup (50 mL) non-fat vanilla yogurt

Wash the quinoa in a sieve under cold running water and drain. In a large pot, combine the quinoa and 4 cups (1 L) of water. Bring to a boil, stirring occasionally. Lower the heat and simmer for 10 minutes. Remove from heat and drain.

In the same large stockpot, combine the cooked quinoa, milk, sugar, salt, cinnamon and cloves and bring to a boil over low heat, stirring occasionally. Turn the heat down to very low and cook an additional 15 minutes, stirring frequently until the mixture is thick and most of the liquid has been absorbed. Stir in the vanilla extract and cook for 5 minutes.

Remove from heat, let cool slightly and stir in the yogurt. Pour the pudding into a casserole dish and sprinkle with additional cinnamon if desired. Serve at room temperature with tropical fruit salad (recipe follows).

Tropical Fruit Salad

We're still amazed that we can be in the middle of a January ice storm, walk into a grocery store and find the exotic fruits we call for in this recipe. There's no need to spend thousands of dollars on a holiday in the sun when you can invite friends over and pretend for the night that you're south of the border, at a fraction of the cost.

2 large yellow bananas or 4 ripe red bananas, sliced
1 large mango, peeled, pit removed, and diced
1 cup (250 mL) fresh pineapple, cut in cubes
1 fresh papaya, peeled, seeds removed, and diced
2 oranges, peel and pith removed, segments
    separated from membrane

Dressing:
3 tbsp (50 mL) unsweetened shredded coconut
1/4 cup (50 mL) lime juice
3 tbsp (50 mL) honey

Put the fruit in a large bowl. Stir the dressing ingredients together and pour over the fruit. Toss gently to distribute dressing. Serve with Quinoa Pudding.

Chapter 4

From Thistles to Shamrocks

English Afternoon Tea

The Perfect Pot of Tea
Afternoon Tea Sandwiches
Oatmeal-Orange Scones
Fresh Strawberry Jam
Princess Pear Brioche
Chocolate-Coconut Meringue Cookies

Scottish Pub Night

Creamy Leek Soup
Shepherd's Pie with Mashed Tatties and Neeps
Copper Pennies and Brussels Sprouts
Baked Apples with Scotch Whisky
Scottish Oatcakes

Irish Celtic Dinner

Tony Bennett's (yes, that's his real name) Irish Stew
Cork Colcannon
Caraway Soda Bread
Galway Gingerbread Cake

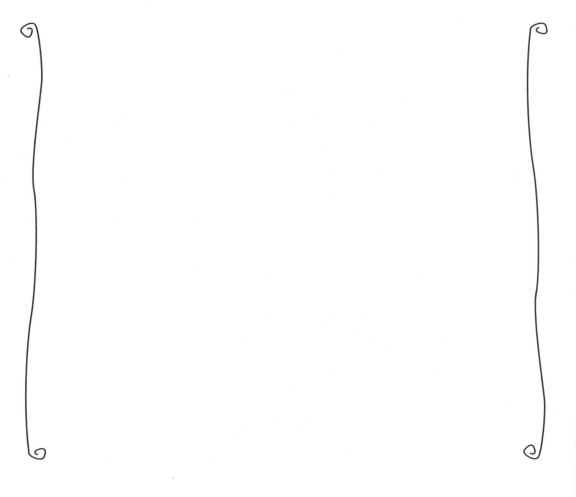

U.K. dishes are notoriously known for their, um, shall we say, filling ingredients? Filling, that is, for the parts of our bodies that we want to stay trim. You know that won't stop us from gobbling up the delightful foods of England, Scotland and Ireland. First stop on our U.K. Express is in England, for an English Afternoon Tea. We begin our adventure with a walk along the Thames. A trip to Cutty Sark in Greenwich is a must, as it is the famous 19th-century vessel that transported the exotic commodity we know as tea. Since we all can't enjoy an afternoon tea in Harrods of London, we decided to give you a recipe for the Perfect Pot of Tea. To go along with it, we've added some Orange-Oatmeal Scones and a Princess Pear Brioche.

"You take the high road and I take the low road, I'll be in Scotland before you." Sound familiar? It is part of a famous song, famous at least to those of us of Scottish descent. Past the castles of England and southern Scotland, our next stop is in Edinburgh. Whether it is a walk around Edinburgh or a hike on the moors, at some point in the day, most visitors and residents will frequent "the local" (local pub that is). We did a little Wendy and Barb makeover and have given you a low-fat, yet smashing, Scottish Pub Night menu that includes a Creamy (yes, creamy) Leek Soup, Shepherd's Pie and Baked Apples with Scotch Whisky. A brisk walk home from the pub will help burn off some of those calories, not from the dinner, but from the beer.

Whether you choose to take the ferry or airplane over to Ireland, read on for our Irish Celtic Dinner. We bet that everyone will admit to having a little Irish spirit in them. What other country has a national holiday that is celebrated in many countries around the world? The legends of leprechauns and Irish clovers (not to mention green beer) are enough for us to be hooked. Whether you desire a terrific football game or a Celtic celebration, we know you will look forward to Tony Bennett's Stew and some Caraway Soda Bread. Satisfying, filling and scrumptiously low-fat. So come on, all ye lads and lassies, put on your Aran sweaters, and let's go.

Menu 1

English Afternoon Tea

The Perfect Pot of Tea
Afternoon Tea Sandwiches
Oatmeal-Orange Scones
Fresh Strawberry Jam
Princess Pear Brioche
Chocolate-Coconut Meringue Cookies

The Perfect Pot of Tea

Serves 10

Per serving:
Calories: 0
(without sugar)
Fat: 0 g

There is a certain art to making tea. Believe us, you can taste the difference when it's made properly. Dig the old silver tea service out of the attic and polish it up. Let's do this right and proper and make Queen Elizabeth II proud.

Bring 10 cups (2.5 mL) of fresh, cold water to a strong, rolling boil in a kettle. Bring a teapot to the kettle (don't carry the kettle to the teapot or the water will stop boiling). Pour 1 cup (250 mL) of the boiling water into the teapot and swirl around to warm the teapot. Discard the water. Put 4 or 5 high-quality tea bags into the teapot and pour the briskly boiling water over. Cover with a lid and a tea cozy or wrap the teapot in a tea towel. Let the tea steep for 3 to 5 minutes.

Serve the tea in cups and saucers with 1% milk, lemon slices and sugar cubes or granulated sugar.

You might want to serve an herbal tea, iced tea or fresh lemonade at your afternoon tea as well.

Afternoon Tea Sandwiches

These sandwiches should be kept small and neat. They are to be eaten in one or two bites, very daintily, so don't overfill them. The possibilities of fillings are endless, so experiment. We have suggested some traditional toppings with a low-fat twist.

Note: Serving size is 3 sandwiches per person. These recipes serve approximately 10 people.

**30 very thin slices of bread, an assortment of
white, whole wheat and pumpernickel**

Cut the crusts off the bread and, with a serrated knife or cookie cutter, cut the bread into different shapes (round, triangles, square or hearts — use your imagination). Wrap the bread in plastic wrap until you are ready to spread with the sandwich toppings.

Bread Moistener:
mustard: Dijon, brown or hot
ultra low-fat mayonnaise
**3 tbsp (50 mL) light cream cheese mixed with 3
    tbsp (50 mL) Yogo Cheese (p. 24)**

Cucumber Topping:
1 English cucumber, peeled and thinly sliced
**thin radish slices, watercress leaves or small
    sprigs of dill for garnish**

**Per serving
(1 sandwich):**

**Calories: 40
Fat: 0.2 g**

Spread a small amount (1/8 to 1/4 teaspoon/0.5 to 1 mL) of the bread moistener on each bread slice. Top with 2 slices of cucumber. Garnish with radish slices, or as desired.

Variation: Mix a small amount of chopped watercress or dill into the cream cheese mixture. Top the bread with the mixture before adding the cucumber.

Salmon Topping:
1 can (7.5 oz/213 g) pink salmon, drained
1 tbsp (15 mL) low-fat mayonnaise
2 tsp (10 mL) lemon juice
1 tbsp (15 mL) snipped fresh dill
salt and pepper to taste
thin radish slices, watercress leaves or small
sprigs of dill for garnish

Per serving
(1 sandwich):

Calories: 56
Fat: 0.8 g

Mash salmon, mayonnaise, lemon juice, dill, salt and pepper in a bowl, using a fork. Stir until well combined and smooth. Spread the salmon on dry bread (it already has mayonnaise in it). Garnish with radish slices, or as desired.

Ham or Smoked Turkey Topping:
10 thin slices lean ham or smoked turkey breast,
chopped
2 tsp (10 mL) chopped fresh parsley
2 tsp (10 mL) low-fat mayonnaise
mustard
1 small tomato, seeded and chopped fine for garnish
1 tbsp (15 mL) cranberry jelly for garnish if using
turkey

Per serving
(1 sandwich):

Calories: 74
Fat: 1.0 g

Mix the ham, parsley and mayonnaise in a small bowl until combined. Spread a small amount of mustard on the bread. Top with ham mixture. Garnish with chopped tomato or cranberry jelly.

Serves 12
Per serving:

Calories: 129
Fat: 2.8 g

Oatmeal-Orange Scones

What would a tea party be without scones? Or a homemade straw-berry jam? Jam is an excellent alternative to butter on toast, muffins and other breads. It is virtually fat free and available in low-sugar varieties.

> 1 1/2 cups (375 mL) all-purpose flour
> 2 tbsp (25 mL) sugar
> 2 tsp (10 mL) baking powder
> 1/2 tsp (2 mL) baking soda
> 1/4 tsp (1 mL) salt
> 2 tbsp (25 mL) soft margarine
> 1 cup (250 mL) quick-cooking oats
> 3 tbsp (50 mL) egg substitute, beaten lightly
> 1/3 cup (75 mL) currants or raisins (if using
>   currants, soak in warm water for 10 minutes,
>   then drain)
> 1 tbsp (15 mL) grated orange peel
> 1/2 cup (125 mL) buttermilk

Preheat oven to 375°F (190°C). Spray a baking sheet with non-stick cooking spray and set aside.

In a large bowl, stir together the flour, sugar, baking powder, baking soda and salt. Add the margarine and combine with a fork until the mixture is crumbly. Stir in the oats. Add the egg substi-tute, currants and orange peel. Stir to combine. Add the butter-milk, a little at a time, mixing just until dough comes together. Gather the dough into a ball and place on a board dusted with flour. Pat dough out to about 1-inch (2.5-cm) thickness and, using a round 2-inch (5-cm) cookie cutter, cut out rounds. Bake for about 20 minutes.

Variation: Pat the dough into a 7-inch (18-cm) circle about 1 inch (2.5 cm) thick and place on baking sheet. Using a sharp knife, cut the dough into 12 wedges. Pull the wedges apart slightly and bake for about 20 minutes.

᦯ ᦯ ᦯ ᦯ ᦯ ᦯ ᦯ ᦯ ᦯ ᦯ ᦯ ᦯ ᦯ ᦯ ᦯ ᦯ ᦯ ᦯ ᦯

Postcards from the Edge

Exercise Tip

To lose weight and body fat, exercise for a longer period of time but at a lower intensity.

**Makes about
1 cup (250 mL)**

**Per serving:
(2 tbsp/30 mL):**

**Calories: 53
Fat: 0.1 g**

Fresh Strawberry Jam

This jam is so easy to make that you may never go back to store-bought again. You can adjust the amount of sugar to suit your taste. If you're already sweet enough, use less.

**3 cups (750 mL) strawberries, washed and hulled
3/4 cup (175 mL) sugar
1 tbsp (15 mL) grated orange zest**

Crush the strawberries with a potato masher or a fork in a medium-sized bowl. This should yield 1 to 1 1/2 cups (250 to 375 mL). Put the strawberries, sugar and orange zest in a non-aluminum saucepan. Bring to a boil over high heat and cook, stirring, until mixture reaches 218°F (103°C) on a candy thermometer, about 5 minutes. Remove from heat and cool. Serve with the scones.

Princess Pear Brioche

Serves 12
Per serving:

Calories: 61
Fat: 0.6 g

These muffins look very pretty when served in brioche molds, so use them if you have them. Using whole wheat flour boosts the nutritional value of these little treats and they're low in fat, so indulge.

> 1 cup (250 mL) all-purpose flour
> 1/2 cup (125 mL) whole wheat flour
> 1 whole egg + 2 egg whites
> 1/2 cup (125 mL) sugar
> 1/4 cup (50 mL) skim milk
> 2 ripe pears, peeled, cored and cut in small dice
> 1 tbsp (15 mL) grated lemon zest

Preheat oven to 350°F (180°C). Spray 12 brioche molds or 2 1/2-inch (100 mL) muffin tins with a non-stick cooking spray and set aside.

In a medium-sized bowl, stir together the all-purpose flour and whole wheat flour.

In a large bowl, beat together the egg, egg whites and sugar until the mixture is pale and fully incorporated, about 4 minutes. Beat in the milk with an electric mixer at low speed. Stir in the flour mixture gradually until mixture is smooth. Add the pears and lemon zest and stir to distribute pears evenly through the batter. Distribute the batter evenly among the molds.

Bake until a toothpick inserted in center comes out clean, about 30 minutes. Serve warm.

Chocolate-Coconut Meringue Cookies

Chocolate and coconut on a low-fat diet? Absolutely. We use cocoa powder and egg whites for the meringues, both which are virtually fat free, so we can indulge in a little of the coconut. These delicate, melt-in-your-mouth cookies won't add an inch to your waist. Too bad King Henry VIII didn't know about them; maybe he wouldn't have been so grumpy.

> 3 large egg whites, at room temperature
> 1/8 tsp 0.5 mL) salt
> 1 cup (250 mL) sugar
> 2 tbsp (25 mL) unsweetened cocoa powder
> 1/2 cup (125 mL) unsweetened shredded coconut
> 1/2 tsp (2 mL) vanilla extract

Preheat oven to 275°F (140°C). Line a baking sheet with parchment and set aside.

In a large, clean bowl, beat the egg whites and salt with an electric mixer until foamy. Slowly add the sugar a little at a time and continue beating until mixture forms soft peaks. Sprinkle the cocoa powder, coconut and vanilla extract over the egg whites and stir gently until just incorporated.

Drop the batter by tablespoonfuls (15 mL), 2 inches (5 cm) apart on the baking sheet. Bake for 30 minutes. Remove and let cool completely.

Menu 2

Scottish Pub Night

Creamy Leek Soup
Shepherd's Pie with Mashed Tatties and Neeps
Copper Pennies and Brussels Sprouts
Baked Apples with Scotch Whisky
Scottish Oatcakes

For Beer Lovers

Beer makes a perfect accompaniment to this hearty fare. Alcohol does have calories and does not have any nutritional value, but it is nice when entertaining to offer a special drink to complement the food and enjoy good company. Our friends at Premier Brands Importers have been kind enough to give us a list of some very special Old Country ales that are now available in North America. Thanks, guys.

McEwans Lager, Scotland (Wendy's dad's favorite)

Younger's Tartan Special, Scotland

Newcastle Brown Ale, England

John Smith's, England

Serves 6

Per serving:
Calories: 107
Fat: 0.6 g

Creamy Leek Soup

Leeks are the national emblem of Wales. That's pretty important status for a vegetable. Leeks have a delectable, subtle flavor. They are grown in sand, so make sure you wash well between their leaves or you'll end up with gritty soup.

> 3 cups (750 mL) leeks (white part only), trimmed,
>   washed well and sliced
> 2 1/2 cups (625 mL) potatoes, peeled and diced
> 3 cups (750 mL) de-fatted chicken stock
> 2 cups (500 mL) evaporated skim milk
> salt and pepper to taste
> snipped fresh chives for garnish

Combine the leeks, potatoes and stock in a large saucepan. Bring to a boil. Lower heat, cover and simmer for 30 minutes. Transfer the soup to a food processor or a blender (you may have to do this in batches) and purée. Pour the soup back into the saucepan, add milk and season to taste. Cook over low heat until just heated through. Ladle into bowls and garnish with chives.

Shepherd's Pie with Mashed Tatties and Neeps

Serves 6

Per serving:
Calories: 321
Fat: 5.0 g

When the cold wind is whipping across the moors, chase the chill away with this hearty, traditional dinner. It's comfort food with a low-fat twist. We add turnips for a change from the usual mashed potato topping. Even the kids will love this simple but tasty dinner.

> 1 lb (500 g) extra-lean ground beef
> 1 1/2 cups (375 mL) diced onion
> 2 cloves garlic, minced
> 2 stalks celery with leaves, chopped
> 3/4 cup (175 mL) de-fatted beef stock
> 3/4 cup (175 mL) canned tomato purée
> 1 tbsp (15 mL) Worcestershire sauce
> 1/2 tsp (2 mL) dried thyme
> 1/4 cup (50 mL) evaporated skim milk
> 1 cup (250 mL) frozen peas
> 2 tbsp (25 mL) sherry or water
> 2 tbsp (25 mL) cornstarch
> salt and pepper to taste

Brown the beef in a large saucepan over medium heat. Drain off any fat. Add onion, garlic and celery and sauté until vegetables start to soften, about 5 minutes. Add the stock, tomato purée, Worcestershire sauce and thyme. Bring to a boil, reduce heat and simmer for 15 minutes. Add the peas and evaporated milk and cook for 2 minutes.

In a small bowl, combine the sherry and cornstarch. Mix until smooth and pour into the beef mixture. Cook, stirring, an additional 2 minutes. Season with salt and pepper and transfer to 6 individual-sized casserole dishes (or 1 large casserole dish).

Preheat oven to 350°F (180°C). Put the potato-turnip topping (recipe follows) into a piping bag and pipe over the meat mixture or spoon over the top, spreading evenly. Bake for 20 to 30 minutes.

Potato and Turnip Topping:
5 large potatoes, peeled and quartered
2 small turnips, peeled and cubed
1 medium onion, diced
1 clove garlic, peeled
1/2 cup (125 mL) skim milk

Put the potatoes, turnips, onion and garlic in a large saucepan. Cover with water and bring to a boil. Cook until tender, about 20 minutes. Drain well, reserving 1/2 cup (125 mL) of the cooking liquid, and return to the saucepan. Set over very low heat. Mash the potato mixture, gradually adding the milk until the mixture is smooth, adding the reserved liquid as needed to make a creamy consistency.

Copper Pennies and Brussels Sprouts

Serves 6

Per serving:
Calories: 60
Fat: 1.5 g

Vegetables are a tasty and nutritious addition to your meals when they are cooked properly. Unfortunately, many of us grew up on overboiled veggies that had lost all resemblance to what they were initially. Beautiful brussels sprouts, like baby cabbages, and bright carrots tossed in a flavorful sauce will make you take a second look at your childhood nemesis.

> 1 lb (500 g) small brussels sprouts, trimmed
> 3 large carrots, peeled and sliced
> 1/2 tsp (2 mL) salt
> 2 tsp (10 mL) soft margarine
> 2 tsp (10 mL) sugar
> 1/4 cup (50 mL) de-fatted beef stock
> 1 tsp (5 mL) dried savory
> fresh ground pepper

With a sharp knife, cut a small "X" in the stem end of each brussels sprout. Put the brussels sprouts, carrots and salt in a saucepan in 3 cups (750 mL) of water, cover and bring to a boil. Lower heat to medium and simmer until tender, about 10 to 12 minutes. Drain.

Melt the margarine in a skillet. Add the sugar. Cook over medium heat until slightly caramelized, about 2 minutes. Add the beef stock, savory and pepper, stirring until combined. Add the vegetables and toss to coat with the sauce. Serve immediately.

Serves 6

Per serving:
Calories: 150
Fat: 0.5 g

Baked Apples with Scotch Whisky

This simple dessert is made special by the addition of whisky. The alcohol cooks off during the baking, so you are left with just the flavor. Pippin apples are the most popular variety of apple in the United Kingdom, but use whatever cooking apple is your favorite.

> **6 pippin apples or firm, tart apples**
> **juice of 1/2 lemon**
> **3 tbsp (50 mL) brown sugar**
> **1/4 tsp (1 mL) cinnamon**
> **1/4 tsp (1 mL) ground nutmeg**
> **1/3 cup (75 mL) raisins**
> **1/3 cup (75 mL) Scotch whisky or apple juice**
> **About 1 cup (250 mL) apple juice**

Preheat oven to 350°F (180°C).

Core the apples, creating a small cavity and making sure not to core all the way through to the bottom. Sprinkle the cavity of each apple with lemon juice.

Mix together the sugar, cinnamon, nutmeg and raisins. Stuff the raisin mixture into the apples and place the apples in a baking dish. Spoon a little of the whisky over the stuffed apples. Pour enough apple juice into the bottom of the baking dish to cover the bottom 1/2 inch (1 cm) of the apples.

Bake until the apples are soft, about 40 minutes. If the filling starts to get too brown, cover the apples with a piece of aluminum foil. Place each of the apples on top of an oatcake (recipe follows) on a serving plate. Spoon apple juice over the apples just before serving to moisten the oatcakes.

Scottish Oatcakes

Serves 12

Per serving:
Calories: 43
Fat: 1.0 g

What Scottish meal would be complete without oatmeal? These little treats make a great addition to the baked apples but can also be eaten on their own with a little honey or jam.

> 1 1/2 cups (375 mL) quick-cooking oats
> 1 tbsp (15 mL) sugar
> 1/8 tsp (0.5 mL) baking soda
> 1 tbsp (15 mL) margarine
> 2/3 cup (150 mL) water
> quick-cooking oats for rolling

Preheat oven to 325°F (160°C). Lightly coat a baking sheet with a non-stick cooking spray and set aside.

Put the 1 1/2 cups (375 mL) oats, sugar and baking soda in a large mixing bowl. In a small saucepan over low heat, heat the margarine and water until the margarine has melted.

Add just enough of the water and margarine mixture to the oat mixture to make a stiff dough. Turn the dough onto a board that has been covered with a sheet of wax paper and sprinkled with oats. With your hands, press the dough out to about 1/4 inch (6 mm) thickness.

Cut the dough into 12 rounds (3 inches/8 cm in diameter) with a cookie cutter, re-rolling if necessary, or cut into squares or triangles with a knife. Carefully lift each oatcake onto the baking sheet. Bake until crisp, about 30 minutes.

Remove from oven and serve alongside Baked Apples with Scotch Whisky (see recipe on page 116) or place one of the apples on top of each oatcake, pouring a little of the hot apple liquid over top to moisten.

Menu 3

Irish Celtic Dinner

Tony Bennett's (yes, that's his real name) Irish Stew
Cork Colcannon
Caraway Soda Bread
Galway Gingerbread Cake

Wine Suggestions

Jackson Triggs, Proprietor's Reserve Meritage, Ontario

For Beer Lovers

Beamish Irish Red Ale

Tony Bennett's (yes, that's his real name) Irish Stew

Serves 6

Per serving:
Calories: 265
Fat: 7.1 g

We named this dish after our friend Tony Bennett, who we knew would appreciate a real rib-sticking, back-home favorite, tweaked the Wendy and Barb low-fat way, of course. We've even added a dark Irish beer to the stew to give it extra richness and taste. We hope our version stands up to the one your Mum made. This stew would be a perfect dinner for a cold winter night: hearty and filling but still low in fat. Although salads are not typically served in Ireland, a salad would be a nice way to round out this menu. Just be sure to use a low-fat dressing.

> 1 tbsp (15 mL) vegetable oil
> 1 1/2 lb (750 g) lean boneless lamb, cut in 1-inch (2.5 cm) cubes
> 3 tbsp (50 mL) all-purpose flour
> 1 large onion, diced
> 3 cups (750 mL) de-fatted chicken stock
> 1 bay leaf
> 1 tsp (5 mL) dried thyme
> 1 tsp (5 mL) dried rosemary
> 3/4 lb (350 g) turnip or rutabaga, peeled and cut in 1/2-inch (1-cm) cubes
> 3 carrots, peeled and thickly sliced
> 1 cup (250 mL) dark Irish ale or Beamish stout
> salt and pepper to taste

1 cup (250 mL) frozen peas
2 tbsp (25 mL) cornstarch
1/4 cup (50 mL) cold water

Heat the oil in a large, heavy saucepan. Dredge the lamb pieces in flour and cook, stirring until browned all over, 5 to 7 minutes. Add the onion and sauté for 1 minute. Add the chicken stock, bay leaf, thyme and rosemary to the saucepan and stir. Bring to a boil, lower heat, cover saucepan and simmer for 1 hour.

After 1 hour, add the turnip, carrots, dark ale and salt and pepper. Cook until vegetables are tender, about 30 minutes. Add the frozen peas to the saucepan and cook for 2 minutes. Mix the cornstarch and water in a small bowl and add it to the stew. Stir until the stew is thickened slightly. Serve immediately.

Cork Colcannon

Serves 6

Per serving:
Calories: 145
Fat: 0.5 g

Cork Colcannon could actually be the national dish of Ireland. Creamy potatoes, flecked with pieces of cabbage and leek, it's simple and scrumptious. This very old dish might just become one of our new favorites.

> 2 lb (1 kg) potatoes, scrubbed, unpeeled, cut in chunks
> 1 to 3 cloves garlic, peeled
> 1 medium head of cabbage, quartered and cored
> 2 leeks (white part only), washed well and sliced
> 1 cup (250 mL) skim milk
> 1/2 tsp (2 mL) mace
> salt and pepper to taste

Bring 2 pots of water to boil over high heat. Put the potatoes and garlic in a medium-sized pot and cook until tender, 15 to 20 minutes. Put the cabbage in a second pot and cook until tender, about 15 minutes.

Put the milk and leeks in a small pot. Bring to a boil, then quickly turn heat down to a simmer and cook just until leeks are tender, 5 to 8 minutes.

Preheat oven to 450°F (230°C). Drain the cabbage and roughly chop it. Set aside. Drain the potatoes and garlic and return them to the pot. Add the mace, salt and pepper, and mash well. Add the cabbage and the leeks with the milk and lightly mash. Stir to combine, being careful not to break up the leeks and cabbage too much. Transfer the mixture to a casserole dish and bake in oven for 5 to 10 minutes to brown slightly, just before serving.

Serves 8

Per serving:
Calories: 134
Fat: trace

Caraway Soda Bread

This is considered a quick bread because the recipe doesn't call for yeast. The secret ingredient is buttermilk, which has a deceiving name since it's actually very low in fat. The buttermilk adds a moistness to the bread while the caraway seeds liven things up with their unmistakable taste and aroma. The original recipe dates back hundreds of years, to when it was cooked in a covered kettle over an open fire.

> 1 cup (250 mL) whole wheat flour
> 1 cup (250 mL) all-purpose flour
> 1 tbsp (15 mL) sugar
> 1 tsp (5 mL) baking powder
> 1/2 tsp (2 mL) baking soda
> 1/2 tsp (2 mL) salt
> 1 tbsp (15 mL) caraway seeds
> 2 egg whites
> 3/4 cup (175 mL) buttermilk

Preheat oven to 375°F (190°C). Lightly spray a baking sheet with non-stick cooking spray and set aside.

In a large bowl, combine the whole wheat flour, all-purpose flour, sugar, baking powder, baking soda, salt and caraway seeds. Mix together well. In a smaller bowl, beat the egg whites lightly. Add the buttermilk to the egg whites, stirring to combine. Add the egg whites to the flour mixture and stir until just combined, being careful not to overmix the dough.

Turn the dough out onto a floured board and shape into a round loaf about 8 inches (20 cm) in diameter. Place the loaf on the baking sheet. With a sharp knife, cut a cross about 1/2 inch (1 cm) deep into the top of the loaf.

Bake for about 40 minutes. Do not let the loaf brown too much. Remove from oven and let cool on a rack before cutting into 8 wedges.

ෆ ෆ ෆ ෆ ෆ ෆ ෆ ෆ ෆ ෆ ෆ ෆ ෆ ෆ ෆ ෆ

Postcards from the Edge

In the Kitchen

Brussels sprouts are high in fiber, carbohydrates, vitamins A and C, potassium and iron. Try topping them with orange or lemon zest, nutmeg, thyme or a little maple syrup.

Cocoa is virtually fat free, which is great news for us chocoholics. It is a fine-textured, unsweetened powder. Dutch process cocoa is the most popular type because it is specially treated to produce a darker, more flavorful cocoa. For a Sunday morning breakfast treat, why not serve hot cocoa instead of coffee? Pour 1 cup (250 mL) skim milk into a saucepan and heat gently almost to the boiling point. In a mug, mix 1 tablespoon (15 mL) cocoa, 1 tablespoon (15 mL) sugar and 1 tablespoon (15 mL) cold milk into a paste. Pour in the hot milk, stir and enjoy.

Scotch whiskies are as diverse as the country itself. Some people swear by single malts while others prefer blends. The north, with its heather-covered hills, produces a whisky with the undertones of the sweet heather itself. Those produced in Islay have the suggestion of smoke and peat. Try a few to discover the intricate differences among them.

There are two types of carbohydrates. Simple carbs in sugar or honey give us quick energy but have little nutritional value and we lose steam quickly after the initial rush. Complex carbs in potatoes, pasta, fruit and vegetables give us vitamins, fiber and the kind of energy we need to keep our bodies and brains active. They make us feel full with less calories and fat and keep our energy levels on an even keel. Good stuff. So go ahead and eat those potatoes; now you know that rumor about them being fattening is an outdated myth.

Serves 12

Per serving:

Calories: 225
Fat: 4.1 g

Galway Gingerbread Cake

In some Irish homes, 5 o'clock tea, or high tea, is still a tradition. It's the perfect time to sit down with a piece of this warm, spicy cake and a hot beverage after a day of hiking in the mountains around the lakes of Killarney or walking the grounds of 16th-century Trinity College.

> 2 cups (500 mL) all-purpose flour
> 2 tsp (10 mL) baking powder
> 1 tsp (5 mL) baking soda
> 1/2 tsp (2 mL) salt
> 2 tsp (10 mL) ground ginger
> 1 tsp (5 mL) cinnamon
> 1/2 tsp (2 mL) ground cloves
> 1/4 cup (50 mL) margarine
> 1/2 cup (125 mL) granulated sugar
> 2 egg whites, lightly beaten
> 1/2 cup (125 mL) molasses
> 1/2 cup (125 mL) warm water
> 2 cups (500 mL) unsweetened applesauce
> 3 tbsp (50 mL) brown sugar
> 1/4 cup (50 mL) chopped walnuts

Preheat oven to 350°F (180°C). Lightly spray a 9x13-inch (3.5 L) baking pan with non-stick cooking spray and set aside.

In a medium-sized bowl, stir together the flour, baking powder, baking soda, salt, ginger, cinnamon and cloves.

In a large bowl, cream together the margarine and granulated sugar. Mix in the egg whites and molasses. Stir the dry ingredients into the egg mixture, alternating with the warm water. Beat until just combined.

Mix together the applesauce and brown sugar in the baking pan, spreading evenly. Sprinkle the chopped walnuts over the applesauce mixture. Spoon the batter on top and bake until a toothpick inserted in center comes out clean, 35 to 40 minutes.

Postcards from the Edge

Just Remember

There are no shortcuts to any place worth going.
— Beverly Sills

Wouldn't it be great if we could take a magic pill one night and wake up with a new body, renewed energy and able to run a marathon? Changing your lifestyle takes hard work and perseverance, but believe us, it's worth it.

You may have to fight a battle more than once to win it.
— Margaret Thatcher

There will be setbacks as you work towards your goal. Old habits die hard. But by easing yourself into exercise slowly and making small changes in your diet, before you know it, the small gains you make every day will make a profound impact on your life.

Chapter 5

Tour de France

North: Alsatian Dinner for Four

La Salade Verte (Belgian Endive Salad)
Coq au Riesling (Chicken in Riesling Sauce)
Oodles of Noodles
Pear and Hazelnut Tarte

Central: Brunch in Burgundy

Omelette with Escargot and Wild Mushrooms
Sorrel and Celeriac Salad
Le Pain (Crusty French Bread)
Potato Galette
Chocolate Soufflés

South: Picnic in Provence

Chèvre Spread with Figs and Pears
Herbes de Provence
Mesclun and Orange Salad
Pissaladière (Onion Tart)
Provençal Seafood Stew
Apple Clafouti

We think of France and we immediately think of romance. A romantic weekend in Paris or lounging on the Côte d'Azur (French Riviera), it doesn't matter, we'd go in a second. We've been told that this country captures the best of everything in the world: the north with its flat fertile lands, the central with its rolling hills, the east with its Alpine ranges and the towering Pyrenees of the south and southwest. With such diversity, how could we choose just 3 regions to indulge ourselves in? Believe us, it was difficult. However, we put on our berets, rolled up our sleeves, sipped a glass of wine and went to work in the kitchen.

We decided to start with a northern Alsatian Dinner for Four. Typically an area not often frequented by North Americans, we were drawn to the wild beauty of the region. Alsace is very close to Germany and the Black Forest, so we offer you a Belgian Endive Salad followed by Chicken in Riesling Sauce, to be topped by our Pear and Hazelnut Tarte.

If we could visit Burgundy, it would be during harvest season — a time when residents gather the ripened grapes to turn into the world-famous Burgundy wines. Here in Burgundy, we choose a brunch that includes Omelettes with Escargot and Wild Mushrooms, Potato Galette and, of course, Chocolate Soufflés. In honor of the capital of the region, try a little Dijon mustard on the Crusty French Bread — a bread that is deliciously different and low-fat, of course.

What would a tour of France be without a stop in Provence? Surrounded by the Alps and on the Italian border, this could possibly be the most romantic place in France. It is here that, in the Middle Ages, troubadours were encouraged to present their courtly love ballads to audiences at the Fortress of Les Baux. Dreamy romantics of today continue this tradition in the most fabled region of France. We choose to provide you with a dreamy picnic spread, suitable for anyone in love. How about a Pissaladière, a Mesclun and Orange Salad and an Apple Clafouti?

You don't have to be in France to experience fabulous French cuisine. We've given you all the tools, now it's just up to you. How about exercising your body afterwards with a romantic stroll? Better yet, hop on your bike and envision you are a part of the Tour de France.

Postcards from the Edge

In the Kitchen

When buying figs, look for those that are soft and have no odor. If they smell sour, they are overripe. Buy them when they are still slightly firm and let them ripen at home at room temperature.

Unlike most other fruit, fruit growers do not leave pears on the tree to ripen. Like figs, choose ones that are firm and let them ripen at home.

Kirsch is a dry, clear brandy made from a special type of cherry. The best kirsch is made from small wild cherries grown in the Black Forest region of Germany. It takes 20 pounds (about 9 kg) of fruit to make one bottle.

Menu 1

North: Alsatian Dinner for Four

La Salade Verte (Belgian Endive Salad)
Coq au Riesling (Chicken in Riesling Sauce)
Oodles of Noodles
Pear and Hazelnut Tarte

Wine Suggestions

Riesling, Leon Beyer, France

Cocktails

For a nice after-dinner drink, try a small glass of Calvados, a cider brandy from the Normandy region in northern France.

La Salade Verte
Belgian Endive Salad

Serves 4

Per serving:
Calories: 58
Fat: 1.9 g

Belgian endive makes a very interesting change in a salad. With a dressing of Champagne vinegar and Dijon mustard, you are almost transported to that country of style and grace, France.

2 bunches watercress
2 heads Belgian endive
2 tbsp (25 mL) canola oil
2 tbsp (25 mL) Champagne vinegar or white wine
2 tbsp (25 mL) vegetable stock
1 tbsp (15 mL) Dijon mustard
1/2 tsp (2 mL) sugar
salt and pepper to taste

Wash the watercress in a large bowl of cold water to remove grit. Drain, remove stems and pat dry.

Cut the stem end of the endive. Wash well and cut into 1/2-inch thick (1-cm) slices. Pat dry. Put the watercress and endive slices in a large bowl.

In a jar with a tight-fitting lid, combine the oil, vinegar, stock, mustard, sugar, salt and pepper. Shake well to combine. Toss the salad with the dressing just before serving.

Coq au Riesling
Chicken in Riesling Sauce

The Alsatian region of France borders Germany. The cuisine here is a little bit more hearty than in other parts of France. This is a classic dish that uses a unique, light-bodied, dry local Riesling quite unlike the much sweeter German Rieslings.

2 tsp (10 mL) vegetable oil
4 chicken breasts, bone in, skinless
1 medium onion, diced
2 medium carrots, peeled and diced
1 medium turnip, peeled and diced
1/2 lb (250 g) mushrooms, quartered
2 tsp (10 mL) chopped fresh thyme
salt and pepper to taste
2 cups (500 mL) de-fatted chicken stock
1 cup (250 mL) Alsatian Riesling
1/2 cup (125 mL) evaporated skim milk

Heat the oil in a non-stick skillet over medium heat. Add the chicken breasts and sauté for about 8 minutes, turning to brown on both sides. Add the onion, carrots, turnip and mushrooms and sauté another 3 minutes, stirring. Add the thyme, salt and pepper, chicken stock and wine. Bring to a boil, cover and reduce heat. Simmer until chicken is cooked through, about 20 to 25 minutes. Stir in the milk and cook until just heated through, about 1 to 2 minutes. Serve immediately over hot noodles.

Oodles of Noodles

Serves 4

Per serving:
Calories: 214
Fat: 1.0 g

Traditionally, you would use egg noodles in this recipe, but with 5 grams of fat per egg yolk, who needs it? Good news. You can now buy egg noodles made without the yolks. Or, just use a wide, flat pasta such as fettuccine or tagliatelle.

> 4 quarts (1 L) water
> 1/2 tsp (2 mL) salt
> 1/2 lb (250 g) dried pasta or noodles
> 2 tbsp (25 mL) de-fatted chicken stock
> 2 tsp (10 mL) caraway seeds

In a large pot, bring the water and salt to a rolling boil. Add the noodles and cook until tender, about 8 to 10 minutes. Drain the noodles, return to the pot and stir in the stock and caraway seeds. Serve immediately.

Pear and Hazelnut Tarte

Sometimes we think we could just skip meals and go straight to dessert. We both have sweet tooths, but we've learned how to eat wisely so that we can indulge in desserts. And, the more we cut down on the fat in the original recipe, the more often we can indulge.

> 1 large egg
> 3/4 cup (175 mL) sugar
> 1 tsp (5 mL) pear liqueur or vanilla extract
> 1/2 cup (125 mL) all-purpose flour
> 1 tsp (5 mL) baking powder
> 1/4 tsp (1 mL) salt
> 1/3 cup (75 mL) chopped hazelnuts or walnuts
> 2 large pears, peeled, cored and diced
> 1% ice cream

Preheat the oven to 350°F (180°C). Lightly spray a 9-inch (22-cm) pie pan with non-stick cooking spray and set aside.

Lightly beat the egg in a large mixing bowl. Add the sugar, liqueur, flour, baking powder, salt, nuts and pears. Stir to combine well.

Spoon the mixture into the prepared pan and press down to make an even layer. Bake for 30 minutes. Remove from oven and let cool slightly. Serve warm with 1% ice cream.

Menu 2

Central: Brunch in Burgundy

Omelette with Escargot and Wild Mushrooms
Sorrel and Celeriac Salad
Le Pain (Crusty French Bread)
Potato Galette
Chocolate Soufflés

Wine Suggestions

Beaujolais, Pisse-Dru, France

Serves 4

Per serving:

Calories: 232
Fat: 4.4 g

Omelette with Escargot and Wild Mushrooms

Yes, we know. Snails. If you don't like them, that's fine: simply add a few more wild mushrooms to this recipe instead. But we think that snails are a delicacy that's definitely worth trying at least once. There's a big world out there offering too many tastes to count. You never know unless you try.

2 tsp (10 mL) olive oil
1 small onion, minced
1 clove garlic, finely minced
1/4 lb (125 g) wild mushrooms (chanterelles,
    oyster or porcini)
1 cup (250 mL) Burgundy
1/2 cup (125 mL) de-fatted chicken stock
2 cans (7 1/2 oz/200 g) giant snails, without shells
salt and pepper to taste
2 tsp (10 mL) cornstarch
1 tbsp (15 mL) water
2 eggs
10 egg whites

Clockwise from top:
Shepherd's Pie with Mashed Tatties and Neeps (p. 113)
Copper Pennies and Brussels Sprouts (p. 115)
Baked Apples with Scotch Whisky (p. 116)
Scottish Oatcakes (p. 117)
Creamy Leek Soup (p. 112)

Heat the oil in a large skillet over medium-high heat. Add the onion and garlic and sauté for 2 minutes. Add the mushrooms and sauté, stirring, 5 more minutes. Add the wine and stock and lower the heat to medium. Cook for 5 minutes. Reduce heat to a simmer and add the snails, salt and pepper; simmer for 3 minutes.

In a cup, mix together the cornstarch and water. Stir into the simmering sauce and cook and stir for 1 minute. Remove skillet from heat, cover and set aside while preparing omelettes.

In a large bowl, beat together the eggs and egg whites. Spray a non-stick skillet lightly with non-stick cooking spray and place over medium heat. Add 1/4 of the eggs and tilt skillet to spread the egg mixture evenly. Cook for 1 minute, gently lifting up one edge of the omelette with a fork and tilting skillet so the uncooked egg runs underneath. Carefully flip the omelette and cook for another 1 to 2 minutes. Remove the omelette to a plate and keep warm in a 200°F (100°C) oven.

Repeat this procedure with the remaining egg mixture until you have 4 omelettes. To assemble, place each omelette on a serving plate, top with 1/4 of the snail mixture and roll, or roll each omelette and spoon the snail mixture over the top.

Clockwise from top:
Apple Clafouti (p. 152)
Provençal Seafood Stew (p. 150)
Pissaladière (Onion Tart) (p. 148)
Chèvre Spread with Figs and Pears (p. 145)
Mesclun and Orange Salad (p. 147)

Sorrel and Celeriac Salad

This salad consists of two unusual vegetables tossed in a creamy dressing made the low-fat way (of course) with non-fat yogurt. Sometimes all you need to perk up that boring salad is the addition of something you haven't tried before.

> **3/4 lb (350 g) fresh sorrel or spinach**
> **1 celeriac (celery root)**
> **1/3 cup (75 mL) fat-free plain yogurt**
> **2 tbsp (25 mL) vegetable stock**
> **1 tbsp (15 mL) tarragon vinegar**
> **1 tbsp (15 mL) Dijon mustard**
> **1 tbsp (15 mL) honey**
> **1 tsp (5 mL) dried tarragon**
> **1 clove garlic, minced**
> **salt and pepper to taste**

Fill a medium-sized bowl with ice water and set aside.

Wash the sorrel well to remove all grit. Trim tough ends, pat dry. Put a pot of water on to boil. Peel the celeriac and cut in half, then cut each half into 1/4-inch slices. Cut the slices into julienne or matchsticks.

When the water is boiling, drop in the celeriac and blanch for 30 seconds. Remove and put in the bowl of ice water. Drain, pat dry and put in a large salad bowl along with the sorrel.

For the dressing, whisk together the yogurt, stock, vinegar, mustard, honey, tarragon, garlic, salt and pepper in a small bowl. Just before serving, toss the dressing with the sorrel and celeriac.

Le Pain
Crusty French Bread

Makes I loaf

Per serving
(I slice):
Calories: 138
Fat: 1.1 g

This crusty loaf of bread has only 1.1 g of fat. The shelf-life of bread is shortened when the fat in it is reduced, so eat up the bread right away. We're sure this won't be a problem; once you make it, you'll see how fast it goes.

> **1 package (1/4 oz/8 g) active dry yeast**
> **1 1/2 cups (375 mL) lukewarm water**
> **1 tsp (5 mL) salt**
> **1 tsp (5 mL) sugar**
> **3 cups (750 mL) bread flour**
> **1 tsp (5 mL) canola oil**
> **1 egg white**
> **1 tbsp (15 mL) water**
> **cornmeal for the baking sheet**

In a small bowl, sprinkle the yeast over the top of 1/2 of the lukewarm water and stir to dissolve yeast. Let stand until the mixture becomes foamy, about 5 minutes

Meanwhile, sprinkle a bread board with flour and a baking sheet with cornmeal and set both aside. Very lightly brush a medium-sized bowl with the oil and set aside.

In a large bowl, combine the remaining lukewarm water, salt and sugar. Pour in the yeast mixture and mix well. Add the flour 1 cup (250 mL) at a time, mixing well after each addition. Transfer the dough to the floured board and knead for 3 minutes. Shape the dough into a ball and put into the oiled bowl, covering the bowl with waxed paper that has been sprayed with non-stick cooking spray. Set in a warm, draft-free place and let the dough rise 1 to 2 hours, until doubled in size.

Punch the dough down and turn out onto the floured board. Knead for 2 minutes, then shape into an oval loaf. Place the loaf onto the baking sheet, covering with waxed paper that has been sprayed with non-stick cooking spray. Let the dough rise for another 1 hour.

Preheat oven to 400°F (200°C). With a very sharp knife or razor blade, cut 3 or 4 slashes across the top of the loaf. Mix the egg white and water together and brush over the top of the loaf. Bake until golden brown and crusty, about 35 to 40 minutes. Cool on wire rack.

෨ ෨ ෨ ෨ ෨ ෨ ෨ ෨ ෨ ෨ ෨ ෨ ෨ ෨ ෨ ෨ ෨

Postcards from the Edge

Living a Healthy Lifestyle

Since we visited France in this chapter, we just have to talk about clothes. We'd bet Parisian women look chic even in old sweatsuits. If you're just getting started on an exercise routine, why not go out and buy some new duds to work out in? Shop for your workout clothes like you would if you were picking out a fancy dress for a party. You don't have to spend a lot of money; pick out a T-shirt in a color you love or a jogging suit that's comfortable and allows you freedom of movement. If you feel good about yourself while you're exercising, you will be more motivated to get out there and MOVE.

Potato Galette

Serves 4

Per serving:
Calories: 114
Fat: 1.3 g

Potatoes are probably the most-favored vegetable in central France, and there are endless recipes for them. Here we offer a classic galette, golden brown and crispy — the simple potato transformed into a masterpiece.

> 1 1/2 lb (750 g) potatoes, peeled and grated
> 1/2 small onion, grated
> pinch of grated nutmeg
> salt and pepper to taste
> 1 tsp (5 mL) olive oil

Put the grated potato in the center of a clean tea towel. Wrap the towel around the potatoes and, holding over the sink, squeeze out as much moisture as you can. Put the potato in a large bowl, add onion, nutmeg, salt and pepper and mix well.

Heat the oil in a large non-stick skillet that has been sprayed with non-stick cooking spray. Place the potato into the skillet and press down with a wooden spoon to make an even layer. Cover and cook potatoes over medium heat for 10 minutes.

Very carefully turn the galette over. The easiest way to do this is to place a large plate over the skillet and turn the skillet upside down, then return the skillet to the heat and slide the galette back in.

Cook the galette for another 10 minutes. Remove to a serving plate and cut into 8 wedges. Keep warm until ready to serve.

Chocolate Soufflés

Most home cooks cringe at the thought of making a soufflé because they believe it will be difficult. That is a myth, as you'll see with this easy yet elegant recipe. Again, cocoa powder comes to the rescue and gives us our chocolate fix without the fat.

> 1 tsp (5 mL) sugar to coat soufflé dishes
> 5 tbsp (75 mL) unsweetened cocoa powder
> 1/4 cup (50 mL) sugar
> 2 tbsp (25 mL) cornstarch
> 1 tsp (5 mL) instant coffee granules
> 1 cup (250 mL) skim milk
> 1 tsp (5 mL) vanilla extract
> 4 egg whites
> 1 tsp (5 mL) cream of tartar
> 1/2 cup (125 mL) sugar

Preheat oven to 350°F (180°C). Lightly spray four 12-ounce (375 mL) soufflé dishes with non-stick cooking spray. Place a small amount of the 1 tsp (5 mL) sugar in each dish, rolling to coat the sides and bottom with the sugar. Set aside.

Mix together the cocoa, 1/4 cup (50 mL) sugar, cornstarch and coffee in a small saucepan. Whisk in the milk and cook over medium heat until the mixture comes to a boil. Cook for 1 minute. Remove from heat and let cool. When the mixture is cool, stir in the vanilla extract.

In a large, clean bowl, beat the egg whites until foamy. Add the cream of tartar and continue beating. Slowly add the 1/2 cup (125 mL) sugar and beat until stiff peaks form. Take 1/4 of the egg white mixture and stir it into the chocolate mixture to lighten it. Fold the chocolate mixture into the egg whites very carefully, mixing until just combined.

Divide the mixture equally among the soufflé dishes, smoothing the tops. Place the soufflé dishes in a large baking dish with sides. Pour hot water into the baking dish around the soufflés until the water comes about 1/3 of the way up the sides of the soufflé dishes. Bake until puffed and set, about 25 minutes. Serve while still warm.

Postcards from the Edge

Exercise Tip

If you vary your exercise routine, you'll be less likely to get bored. Learning a new sport or trying a new activity might be just the trick to jumpstart your routine again.

Menu 3

South: Picnic in Provence

Chèvre Spread with Figs and Pears
Herbes de Provence
Mesclun and Orange Salad
Pissaladière (Onion Tart)
Provençal Seafood Stew
Apple Clafouti

 # Wine Suggestions

Fortant de France, Chardonnay, France

Chèvre Spread with Figs and Pears

Serves 8

Per serving:
Calories: 115
Fat: 3.7g

Here it is again, the irreplaceable Yogo Cheese. We don't believe you should have to give up everything while trying to eat low-fat. By cutting the amount of goat cheese used and substituting the Yogo Cheese, you can enjoy this smooth, creamy spread on succulent fruit and not miss a thing.

> juice of 1/2 lemon
> 2 fresh, firm pears, quartered
> 2 fresh figs, quartered
> 1/2 cup (125 mL) Yogo Cheese (see page 24 for recipe)
> 4 oz (125 g) chèvre or other goat cheese
> 2 tbsp (25 mL) honey
> 1 tbsp (15 mL) fresh lemon juice
> 1 tbsp (15 mL) herbes de Provence (store bought or homemade, recipe follows)
> lemon zest curls for garnish

Pour the juice of 1/2 a lemon into a bowl of water and add the pears. Refrigerate the pears and figs in separate bowls while preparing the dip.

In a medium-sized bowl, mix together the Yogo Cheese, chèvre, honey and the 1 tablespoon (15 mL) of lemon juice, blending until smooth. Add the herbes de Provence and mix until just incorporated. To serve, spoon approximately 1 tablespoon (15 mL) of spread on each fruit quarter. Garnish with a curl of lemon zest.

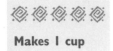

Makes 1 cup

Herbes de Provence

Lavender, which grows wild during the summer in Provence, is the secret ingredient in this mix. Lavender is available in health food stores, bulk food stores and craft stores that carry potpourri mix. This fragrant combination of herbs goes well with lamb, chicken or fish, but don't just save it for the kitchen. Make a small sachet out of cheesecloth, fill it with a couple of spoonfuls of this mixture and place it in your lingerie drawer for a wonderful scent.

> 1/4 cup (50 mL) dried basil
> 1/4 cup (50 mL) dried rosemary
> 3 bay leaves, finely ground
> 3 tbsp (50 mL) dried thyme
> 3 tbsp (50 mL) dried oregano
> 1 tbsp (15 mL) dried lavender
> 1 tsp (5 mL) dried coriander
> 1/2 tsp (2 mL) ground cloves

Combine all the ingredients in a bowl and stir to combine well. Store in an airtight container.

Mesclun and Orange Salad

Mesclun is a Provençal blend of tender young salad greens that are now available in most grocery stores pre-mixed and ready to go. These chic greens and homemade dressing (so easy you'll never go back to the bottled variety) will make you say "oui" to eating your greens.

> 6 cups (1.5 L) mesclun salad greens (mixed tender young greens)
> 2 large seedless oranges
> 2 tbsp (25 mL) white wine vinegar
> 2 tbsp (25 mL) orange juice
> 1 tbsp (15mL) vegetable oil
> 1 tbsp (15 mL) Dijon mustard
> 1 clove garlic, minced
> 1 tsp (5 mL) grated orange zest
> salt and pepper to taste

Put the greens in a large bowl. With a sharp knife, trim and peel the skin and white pith from the oranges. Cut each orange into 1/4-inch (6-mm) slices and add to the greens.

In a jar with a tight-fitting lid, combine the vinegar, orange juice, oil, mustard, garlic, orange zest, salt and pepper, shaking well to combine. Just before serving, pour the dressing over the greens and toss gently.

Serves 12

Per serving:

Calories: 154
Fat: 3.5

Pissaladière
Onion Tart

Slow-cooked caramelized onions on a crisp, flaky crust: this tart is a classic French tradition. The garnish of anchovies and olives is standard but, as in every recipe, omit them if they're not to your taste. This dish makes a tasty appetizer when served at room temperature.

> **Crust:**
> 1 tsp (5 mL) sugar
> 2/3 cup (150 mL) lukewarm water
> 1 package (1/4 oz/8 g) active dry yeast
> 2 1/2 cups (625 mL) all-purpose flour
> 1 tsp (5 mL) salt
> 1 large egg, beaten
> 1 tbsp (15 mL) olive oil

Dissolve the sugar in the lukewarm water. Sprinkle the yeast over the top of the lukewarm water and let stand until mixture becomes foamy, about 5 minutes.

Combine the flour and salt in a large bowl. Add the egg, oil and yeast mixture and stir. Use your hands to incorporate the wet and dry ingredients and keep working the dough in bowl until smooth, about 5 minutes. Cover the bowl with waxed paper sprayed with non-stick cooking spray and put in a warm place free from drafts for an hour or until it has doubled in bulk. Meanwhile, lightly spray a 10-inch (25-cm) tart pan with a non-stick cooking spray and set aside.

Preheat the oven to 350°F (180°C). Punch down the dough and turn out of the bowl onto a lightly floured surface. Knead the dough briefly, then place in the tart pan. Push the dough out to edges of pan. Bake the crust for 10 minutes. Remove pan from oven.

Meanwhile, prepare filling:

> 1 tbsp (15 mL) olive oil
> 1 tbsp (15 mL) vegetable stock
> 2 cloves garlic, minced
> 2 lb (1 kg) white or yellow onions, thinly sliced
> salt to taste
> 1 bay leaf
> 1 tsp (5 mL) dried thyme
> 1 tsp (5 mL) dried rosemary
> 8 anchovy fillets, soaked in milk for 15 minutes,
>   then drained
> 12 small black olives

Heat the oil and stock in a large skillet. Add the garlic, onions, salt, bay leaf, thyme and rosemary. Stir to combine ingredients; cover and cook over low heat for about 45 minutes, stirring occasionally and adding a little water if the onion start to stick to skillet.

Preheat oven to 475°F (245°C).

To assemble: Spread the onion mixture over prebaked crust, arrange anchovy fillets and olives over the onions. Bake for 10 to 15 minutes. Remove from oven, cut into wedges and serve warm.

Serves 8

Per serving:
Calories: 240
Fat: 5.1 g

Provençal Seafood Stew

This is another of those classic dishes that varies from household to household. Prepared with classic Provençal flavorings like saffron and orange zest, it is a seafood lover's dream. Although this recipe calls for a lot of ingredients, it's really an easy dish to make.

2 tbsp (25 mL) olive oil
2 leeks (white part only), trimmed, washed well and sliced
1 large onion, halved and thinly sliced
2 large carrots, peeled and sliced
2 cloves garlic, minced
1/4 cup (50 mL) chopped fresh parsley
2 bay leaves
2 sprigs fresh thyme, chopped
1 piece dried orange zest (optional)
1 cup (250 mL) dry white wine
2 tbsp (25 mL) Pernod (optional)
3 cups (750 mL) fish stock, water or bottled clam juice
1 can (19 oz/540 mL) plum tomatoes, with juice
1 tsp (5 mL) saffron threads or turmeric
1 1/2 lb (750 g) firm-fleshed fish (monkfish, halibut, sea bass, cod or snapper), cleaned and cut into 1 1/2-inch (4-cm) squares
1/2 lb (250 g) shrimp, shelled and deveined
1/2 lb (250 g) mussels, cleaned and beards removed
1/2 lb (250 g) clams, cleaned

salt and pepper to taste
chopped fresh parsley for garnish

Heat the oil in a large stockpot. Add the leeks, onion, carrots and garlic, sautéing over medium heat for 1 minute. Add the 1/4 cup (50 mL) parsley, bay leaves, thyme and orange zest and sauté for 5 minutes. Add the wine, Pernod, stock, tomatoes and saffron and bring to a boil. Reduce heat and simmer for 30 minutes.

Add the fish and continue to simmer for 5 minutes. Add the shrimp, mussels and clams, salt and pepper and cook, covered, for an additional 5 minutes. Before serving, discard any mussels or clams that have not opened. Garnish with additional chopped fresh parsley.

ᕤ ᕤ ᕤ ᕤ ᕤ ᕤ ᕤ ᕤ ᕤ ᕤ ᕤ ᕤ ᕤ ᕤ ᕤ ᕤ ᕤ ᕤ

Postcards from the Edge

Just Remember

The word impossible is not in my dictionary.
— Napoleon Bonaparte

Keep telling yourself that you can do anything. Visualize what you'd like to look like; repeat mantras to yourself that you are getting slimmer or that you can walk that extra half mile. These may sound like silly little tricks, but they work.

Serves 6

Per serving:

Calories: 216
Fat: 1.7 g

Apple Clafouti

The texture of this moist cake borders on that of a pudding. Many types of fruits are used in classic clafoutis; the original recipe, from Limousin, uses fresh black cherries. The kirsch adds a distinctive flavor to the cake, but you could use Calvados if you prefer an apple flavor.

2 tbsp (25 mL) kirsch or brandy
2 tbsp (25 mL) lemon juice
2 tbsp (25 mL) brown sugar
3 apples, peeled, cored and sliced
1 whole egg + 1 egg white
2 tbsp (25 mL) granulated sugar
3/4 cup (175 mL) skim milk
1 tsp (5 mL) vanilla extract
1 1/2 cups (375 mL) all-purpose flour

Preheat oven to 350°F (180°C). Lightly spray a 10-inch (25 cm) pie or tart pan with non-stick cooking spray and set aside.

Combine the kirsch, lemon juice and brown sugar in a medium-sized bowl. Add the apples and toss to coat.

In a second bowl, combine the egg, egg white, granulated sugar, milk and vanilla extract. Beat the ingredients to combine well. Sift the flour into the egg mixture and mix just until the flour is incorporated. Fold in the apple mixture.

Pour the batter into the pan. Bake until nicely browned and a toothpick inserted in center comes out clean, about 45 minutes.

Chapter 6

The Lean Tower of Pisa Tour

North: The Pleasures of Piedmont

That's Amore Artichoke Soup
Milanese Risotto
Parma Pork Medallions
Sophia's Spinach with Pine Nuts
Amaretti-Stuffed Peaches

Central: When in Rome

Bellissima Bruschetta
Mama Marranca's Minestrone
Rotini with Ricotta Arrabbiata Sauce
Arugula Salad with Walnut Balsamic Dressing
Melon Salad with Anise Cookies

South: Sizzlin' Sicilians

Palermo Pizza
Pregiata Penne with Seafood Sauce
Broccoli Raab
Cappuccino
Almond Biscotti

Mama Mia Italy. Land of romance, where we can glide down canals in gondolas with dark-haired men serenading us with classic love ballads. Or dine alfresco under the stars on the shore of the Mediterranean Sea. From north to south, Italy offers a diverse cuisine — there is much more to discover than ravioli and spaghetti. And we can be transported to Italy for an evening by preparing these authentic recipes.

We've divided our recipes into three regions: the north, central and south. The Wendy and Barb Express begins in the northern city of Piedmont. Piedmont lures tourists with that highest of Alpine peaks, Mont Blanc. The northern region typically consumes more rice than the Italian staple of pasta. Rice is a great side dish with our Parma Pork Medallions. We highly recommend that you try our Milanese Risotto. We know that risotto takes a long time to cook, but it's well worth it. While you're stirring the risotto, invite everyone into the kitchen and enjoy great conversation and great company.

The grandeur of central Italy leads us to Rome, home of the Colosseum, the Pantheon and the Forum. We took to heart the saying, "When in Rome, do as the Romans do." It inspired us to create our Bellissima Bruschetta, Mama Marranca's Minestrone and our Rotini with Ricotta Arrabbiata Sauce. If you're not up to making the whole spread, the minestrone soup with some salad and bruschetta make a great meal on its own.

Last but certainly not least, we take you to the south of Italy, right onto the fabled island of Sicily. A unique and diverse land where you can ski down a volcano or swim surrounded by almond trees, the south of Italy is famous for its pizza. Wendy and Barb had to jump on this bandwagon and create a mouth-watering, low-fat Palermo Pizza recipe. We also offer you Pregiata Penne with Seafood Sauce and Broccoli Raab. Almond Biscotti with a cappuccino is the clincher. Want to really end on an Italian note? Run yourself a hot bath with some Epsom salts and relax. The Caesars used to soak in hot mineral springs called grottoes, trying to burn off those dinner calories. Wendy and Barb weren't around back then.

Menu 1

North: The Pleasures of Piedmont

That's Amore Artichoke Soup
Milanese Risotto
Parma Pork Medallions
Sophia's Spinach with Pine Nuts
Amaretti-Stuffed Peaches

Wine Suggestions

Campofiorin, Masi, Italy

That's Amore Artichoke Soup

Serves 4

Per serving:
Calories: 156
Fat: 0.5 g

In the northern part of Italy, you will find fabulous outdoor farmers' markets. The soil is so rich in this part of the country that all kinds of vegetables grow extremely well. We have suggested frozen artichoke hearts for this recipe because we know how intimidating fresh artichokes look, although by all means use fresh if you like.

>   1 small onion, diced
>   2 packages (9 oz/270 g) frozen artichoke hearts,
>   thawed
>   1 1/2 cups (375 mL) skim milk
>   1 tsp (5 mL) salt
>   1 tsp (5 mL) sugar
>   1 cup (250 mL) evaporated skim milk
>   fresh ground pepper
>   chopped fresh parsley for garnish
>   4 lemon wedges for garnish

Combine the onion, artichoke hearts, skim milk, salt and sugar in a medium-sized saucepan. Heat until the mixture is just simmering, making sure it does not boil. Cook for 20 minutes over low heat. Remove saucepan from heat and allow to cool slightly.

Transfer the soup to a food processor or blender and purée. Return the purée to saucepan and reheat over very low heat. Stir evaporated skim milk into purée and whisk to combine. Cook until just heated through. Ladle into serving dishes and top with chopped parsley. Serve lemon wedges on the side.

Serves 4

Per serving:
Calories: 352
Fat: 2.7 g

Milanese Risotto

Here is a classic risotto, smooth and creamy, with a subtle hint of that exotic spice, saffron. If you find saffron a bit too pricey, substitute turmeric. It will still give a wonderful color and taste to the dish but is easier on the pocketbook. Or save this recipe for a special occasion and go all out.

>   4 cups (1 L) de-fatted chicken stock
>   2 tsp (10 mL) olive oil
>   1 large onion, finely minced
>   1 1/2 cups (375 mL) arborio rice
>   1/4 tsp (1 mL) saffron threads
>   3/4 cup (175 mL) white wine
>   salt and pepper to taste
>   1/4 cup (50 mL) reduced-fat Parmesan cheese

Bring the chicken stock to a boil in a medium-sized saucepan. Reduce heat to just maintain a simmer. In a large saucepan, heat the oil over medium heat and add the onion. Sauté the onion for 3 minutes. Add the rice and sauté for 2 minutes, being careful not to brown the rice. Add the saffron and the wine and cook over medium heat, stirring constantly, about 10 minutes to reduce the liquid by half.

   Start adding the stock, about 1/2 cup (125 mL) at a time, stirring constantly until the stock is absorbed by the rice before adding another 1/2 cup (125 mL). This process will take 15 to 20 minutes, after which time the rice should be tender and all the liquid absorbed. Remove risotto from heat, season with salt and pepper and stir in the Parmesan. Serve immediately.

Parma Pork Medallions

Serves 4

Per serving:
Calories: 128
Fat: 4.8 g

You will find heartier, peasant-style meat dishes in the north of Italy than in other parts of the country. In this recipe, however, the pork is cooked in a delicate sauce flavored with rosemary and balsamic vinegar, which makes it perfect for the most elegant dinner party.

> 2 tsp (10 mL) olive oil
> 12 medallions cut from pork tenderloin, pounded
>   to 1/2-inch (1-cm) thickness
> salt and pepper to taste
> 1 cup (250 mL) de-fatted chicken stock
> 3 tbsp (50 mL) balsamic vinegar
> 3 sprigs fresh rosemary

Heat the oil in a large non-stick skillet. Add the medallions (you may have to cook them in two batches) and brown them on both sides over medium-high heat, about 3 minutes per side. Remove medallions to a platter and season with the salt and pepper.

Add the stock to skillet, scraping up any browned pieces of meat from the bottom of the skillet. Add the vinegar and rosemary and bring to a boil. Reduce heat to low and return medallions to skillet. Cover and simmer for 20 minutes, turning medallions occasionally, until meat is tender and sauce has reduced. Remove the rosemary sprigs and transfer medallions to serving plates. Pour the sauce over the medallions and serve immediately.

Serves 4

Per serving:
Calories: 59
Fat: 2.3 g

Sophia's Spinach with Pine Nuts

Sophia Loren has to be one of our favorite actresses. She is beautiful, confident and an amazing cook, so we hear. We honor her with this recipe. We know that sometimes just plain veggies don't cut it, so here we've jazzed up spinach with garlic, lemon juice and pine nuts. Now the ordinary becomes extraordinary.

1 1/2 lb (750 g) spinach
2 tsp (10 mL) olive oil
1 clove garlic, finely minced
1 tbsp (15 mL) pine nuts, coarsely chopped
1 tbsp (15 mL) lemon juice
1/4 tsp (1 mL) ground nutmeg
salt and pepper to taste

Remove tough stems from the spinach and wash well in cold water. Do not dry the spinach. Put the spinach with water still clinging to leaves in a large saucepan and cook, covered, over medium heat until spinach is wilted, about 3 to 5 minutes. Put the spinach in a colander and press out excess water with the back of a wooden spoon. Coarsely chop spinach and set aside.

In a non-stick skillet, heat the oil over low heat. Add the garlic and sauté for 1 minute. Add the spinach and cook until most of the moisture has evaporated, about 3 to 5 minutes. Transfer to a serving bowl and add the pine nuts, lemon juice, nutmeg, salt and pepper. Toss to combine. Serve hot.

Amaretti-Stuffed Peaches

Serves 4

Per serving:
Calories: 111
Fat: 2.1 g

Amaretti are delicious little almond-flavored cookies famous throughout Italy. Here we turn them into a crispy topping for succulent baked peaches, a light but satisfying end to our meal.

> 4 large freestone peaches
> 1/2 cup (125 mL) crushed amaretti cookies
> 2 tbsp (25 mL)sugar
> 2 tbsp (25 mL) grated lemon zest
> 1 egg white
> 1 tbsp (15 mL) lemon juice
> 1 tbsp (15 mL) water
> 1 tsp (5 mL) sugar

Preheat oven to 350°F (180°C). Peel and halve the peaches. Remove pits. Scoop a small amount of peach pulp out of each half, leaving a 1/2-inch-thick (1 cm) shell. Put pulp in a bowl. Add the crushed amaretti cookies, 2 tbsp (25 mL) sugar, lemon zest, egg white and lemon juice to the peach pulp. Stir to combine ingredients.

Place the peach halves in a shallow baking pan and fill each half with some of the amaretti mixture. Sprinkle the water evenly over stuffed peaches; then sprinkle 1 teaspoon (5 mL) sugar evenly over them. Bake until fruit is tender and a slight crust has formed on the top, about 20 minutes. Serve with a spoonful of vanilla yogurt or low-fat ice cream.

Menu 2

Central: When in Rome

Bellissima Bruschetta
Mama Marranca's Minestrone
Rotini with Ricotta Arrabbiata Sauce
Arugula Salad with Walnut Balsamic Dressing
Melon Salad with Anise Cookies

 # Wine Suggestions

Ricolsi, Chianti, Italy

Bellissima Bruschetta

Serves 6

Per serving:
Calories: 35
Fat: 0.9 g

By now you probably know that when we were trying to find low-fat products in the grocery store when we started our low-fat crusade, they just weren't available. So what did we do? We made our own. In this recipe, we use our bruschetta, with tomatoes, onion and spices. Yum. And no fat. Hurrah!

> **1/2 loaf Italian bread**
> **1 container (8 oz/227 g) Wendy and Barb's You**
> **Won't Believe This is Low-Fat Bruschetta**

Preheat oven to 400°F (200°C). Slice the bread into six 1/2-inch-thick (1-cm) slices. Place on a baking sheet and toast in oven until golden brown. Remove from oven and top each slice with 2 teaspoons (10 mL) bruschetta. Place back on baking sheet and bake for 3 to 5 minutes. Serve immediately as an appetizer or with Mama Marranca's Minestrone (recipe follows).

Serves 6 to 8

Per serving:
Calories: 202
Fat: 2.0 g

Mama Marranca's Minestrone

There are probably as many recipes for minestrone as there are people in Italy. Every family has its favorite. Here we borrow a recipe from our trusted expert on Italian cuisine, Mary Marranca. Filled with an array of veggies, beans and macaroni, this soup makes a wonderful lunch all on its own.

2 tsp (10 mL) olive oil
2 cloves garlic, minced
2 large onions, diced
2 stalks celery, sliced
1 can (5 1/2 oz/156 mL) tomato paste
1 can (19 oz/540 g) plum tomatoes, crushed, with
    their juice
8 cups (2 L) de-fatted chicken stock
2 cups (500 mL) water
1/4 head cabbage, shredded
2 carrots, peeled and sliced
1/2 tsp (2 mL) salt
1/2 tsp (2 mL) dried oregano
1/4 tsp (1 mL) pepper
1 medium zucchini, sliced
1 can (14 oz/398 g) red kidney beans, drained
2 tbsp (25 mL) chopped fresh basil
1 cup (250 mL) macaroni or other small pasta
chopped fresh basil or parsley for garnish

Heat the oil in a large stockpot. Add the garlic, onions and celery and sauté over medium heat for 3 to 5 minutes. Stir in the tomato paste, tomatoes, stock, water, cabbage, carrots, salt, oregano and pepper. Stir to combine ingredients. Bring to a boil, cover and reduce heat. Simmer for 1 hour. Add zucchini, beans, 2 tablespoons (25 mL) basil and the pasta and cook for 8 to 10 minutes. Ladle into soup bowls and garnish with chopped fresh basil.

Postcards from the Edge

In the Kitchen

Looking for an easy way to peel garlic? Simply put an unpeeled garlic clove on a cutting board and with the side of a large knife, press down firmly on the clove until you feel it crush slightly. Slip the skin off the clove, and you're in business.

Arborio rice is a short, round grain that is best suited to making risotto because of its capacity to absorb liquid. It is also a very starchy rice that adds a natural creaminess to any dish you use it in.

Rotini with Ricotta Arrabbiata Sauce

Now we're talkin' spicy. Arrabbiata sauce is a heavily seasoned tomato sauce that we have tamed down here with non-fat ricotta cheese. The cheese adds a smooth contrast and certain richness to the dish, but by choosing a ricotta made with skim milk, the sauce is kept low in fat.

> 2 tsp (10 mL) olive oil
> 2 cloves garlic, finely minced
> 1 large onion, finely chopped
> 1/2 tsp (2 mL) hot red pepper flakes
> 1 can (19 oz/540 g) plum tomatoes, crushed, with
>   their juice
> 1 tsp (5 mL) dried basil
> 1/2 tsp (2 mL) dried oregano
> 1 bay leaf
> salt and pepper to taste
> 1 lb (500 g) rotini
> 1 cup (250 mL) non-fat ricotta cheese
> chopped fresh basil for garnish

Heat the oil in a large saucepan. Add the garlic, onion and red pepper flakes and sauté over medium heat for 3 minutes. Add the tomatoes, dried basil, oregano, bay leaf, salt and pepper. Cook over medium-low heat for about 15 minutes or until sauce has thickened slightly. Remove the bay leaf.

Bring a large stockpot of water to a boil and cook rotini until tender but still firm, about 10 minutes. Drain the rotini and add to saucepan; toss rotini with sauce. Add the ricotta and toss lightly again. Sprinkle with the chopped fresh basil and serve immediately.

Postcards from the Edge

Living a Healthy Lifestyle

If you've decided you want to make some changes in your lifestyle, remember the old saying "Rome wasn't built in a day." Small steps add up to giant leaps. These tips will get you started:

1. Add some fruit, vegetables and whole grain products to your daily intake of food.
2. Switch to low-fat products, for example, skim or 1% milk instead of whole milk, and low-fat yogurt, ice cream or puddings instead of high-fat desserts.
3. Cut down your portion sizes. Instead of eating 3 large meals, eat 5 smaller ones.
4. Listen to your body. Feed it when it's hungry, rest it when it's tired and move it even when it feels sluggish. You will get more energy, we promise.
5. Ease yourself into exercise. Go for a walk a couple of times a week. When you're ready, pick up the pace a bit, add an extra day of exercise to your routine and make your walks a little longer.

Serves 6

Per serving:
Calories: 42
Fat: 1.0 g

Arugula Salad with Walnut Balsamic Dressing

A bitter, peppery green, arugula makes a nice addition to a salad. There are many different types of balsamic vinegar, some being aged longer than others, so shop around to find one you like. The addition of the walnuts adds a nice crunchiness to this salad, but don't use many; although nuts are nutritious they are high in fat.

1 small bunch arugula
1 small head red or green leaf lettuce
1 small head radicchio
1/3 cup (75 mL) chopped walnuts, lightly toasted
2 tbsp (25 mL) finely minced onion
1/2 cup (125 mL) vegetable or de-fatted chicken
   stock
2 tbsp (25 mL) balsamic vinegar
salt and pepper to taste

Separate the lettuce into leaves, wash and dry. Tear the leaves into bite-sized pieces into a salad bowl. Whisk together the walnuts, onion, stock, vinegar, salt and pepper. Pour over the greens and toss gently.

Melon Salad with Anise Cookies

The anisette in this recipe is what makes this fruit salad so unusual. It has a light licorice flavor that is refreshing after a meal, and with its digestive qualities, it's a good dish to serve after the main meal. The crunchy cookies that accompany our salad are made with anise seeds, the spice used to make anisette.

Melon Salad:
3 small melons (honeydew or cantaloupe, or a
  mix of the two)
1/3 cup (75 mL) lemon juice
1/3 cup (75 mL) honey
1 tbsp (15 mL) anisette (optional)

Cut the melons in half and remove seeds. Using a baller, scoop melon into a large bowl. Mix together the lemon juice, honey and anisette and pour over the fruit. Refrigerate covered for 1 hour before serving.

Anise Cookies:
2 cups (500 mL) all-purpose flour
1 tsp (5 mL) baking powder
1 tsp (5 mL) crushed anise seeds
1/4 tsp (1 mL) salt
3/4 cup (175 mL) sugar
3 tbsp (50 mL) vegetable shortening
1 egg + 2 egg whites, lightly beaten
1/8 tsp (0.5 mL) anise extract or 1 tsp (5 mL)
  anisette

Makes about
40 cookies

Per serving:
(1 cookie):
Calories: 49
Fat: 1.0 g

Preheat the oven to 375°F (190°C). Spray a baking sheet with non-stick cooking spray and set aside.

Combine the flour, baking powder, anise seeds, salt and sugar in a large bowl. Mix well. Add the shortening and blend with a pastry blender or mixer to incorporate well. Stir in the egg, egg whites and anise extract and mix together to form a stiff dough.

Turn the dough out onto a lightly floured board and divide in half. Roll out 1/2 of the dough to 1/4-inch (6 mm) thickness and cut out rounds with a 2-inch (5-cm) cookie cutter or a glass. Repeat with the remaining dough. Place the cookies on the baking sheet and bake for 10 to 12 minutes. Remove the cookies to a wire rack to cool. Serve with melon salad.

Postcards from the Edge

Entertaining

What could be easier than having an Italian-themed dinner party? All you need is a red-and-white-checked tablecloth, a few candles placed in old wicker-covered Chianti bottles and a little Frank Sinatra or Tony Bennett on the stereo.

Menu 3

South: Sizzlin' Sicilians

Palermo Pizza
Pregiata Penne with Seafood Sauce
Broccoli Raab
Cappuccino
Almond Biscotti

Wine Suggestions

Valpolicella, Folanari, Italy

Palermo Pizza

When we in North America think of Italian food, pizza is one of the first dishes to come to mind. Although tomatoes, a main ingredient in pizza, weren't introduced to Italy until the 16th century, the Italians were eating topped flat breads called focaccia long before that. As much as we love focaccia, we're sure thankful to the Italians for the traditional tomato sauce-topped pizza we know today.

Crust:
1 cup (250 mL) lukewarm water
1 package (1/4 oz/8 g) active dry yeast
1/8 tsp (0.5 mL) salt
2 cups (500 mL) all-purpose flour
1 1/2 cups (375 mL) whole wheat flour

In a small bowl, combine the water and salt. Sprinkle the yeast over the top of the water and stir to dissolve yeast. Let stand until mixture becomes foamy, about 5 minutes.

In a large bowl, stir together the all-purpose flour and the yeast mixture. Mix until smooth. Add 1 1/4 cups (300 mL) of the whole wheat flour and mix. Add just enough of the remaining flour to form a soft dough. Turn the dough out onto a lightly floured surface and knead until smooth and elastic, about 5 minutes.

Place the dough in a lightly oiled bowl, cover with waxed paper that has been sprayed with non-stick cooking spray and let it rise in a warm place free from drafts for 2 hours. Punch dough down. Turn out onto a lightly floured board and knead for 2 minutes. Place back in bowl, cover and let rise again for 1 hour.

Lightly spray a pizza pan or round baking sheet with non-stick cooking spray. Turn the dough out onto the floured board again and shape into a 12-inch (30-cm) circle. Place the dough onto the prepared pan and set aside while preparing the topping.

Topping:
2 tsp (10 mL) olive oil
1 red pepper, seeded and cut into thin strips
1 yellow pepper, seeded and cut into thin strips
1 green pepper, seeded and cut into thin strips
1 onion, halved, then sliced into very thin crescents
salt and pepper to taste
6 slices (1/4 inch/6 mm thick) fresh skim mozzarella

Heat the oil in a large skillet over medium heat. Add the peppers and onion and sauté for 5 to 8 minutes, stirring, until vegetables have softened. Season with salt and pepper and set aside.

Preheat oven to 450°F (230°C). When vegetables have cooled slightly, spread them over the pizza dough. Top the vegetables with slices of mozzarella. Bake pizza until crust is brown and cheese is melted, about 10 to 15 minutes. Remove from oven and cut in wedges.

Serves 6

Per serving:
Calories: 398
Fat: 3.8 g

Pregiata Penne with Seafood Sauce

Sicily is a beautiful, mountainous island surrounded by waters rich with seafood, so it's no wonder the cooking of the south is based largely on the treasures of the sea. Tube-type pastas are also favored here. We have suggested you use penne in this recipe, but there is an endless assortment of pastas to choose from, so have fun with it.

2 tsp (10 mL) olive oil
1 large onion, finely diced
1 clove garlic, minced
1 can (28 oz/796 mL) plum tomatoes, crushed,
  with their juice
2 tbsp (25 mL) chopped fresh basil
2 tbsp (25 mL) capers
2 tbsp (25 mL) pitted black olives, chopped
3/4 lb (375 g) small shrimp, shelled and deveined
3/4 lb (375 g) bay scallops
salt and pepper to taste
1 lb (500 g) penne
chopped fresh parsley for garnish

Put a large pot of water on to boil for pasta. In a large skillet, heat the oil over medium heat. Add the onion and garlic and sauté for 1 minute. Add the tomatoes with their juice and the basil. Lower the heat and simmer sauce for 8 to 10 minutes. Add the capers, olives, shrimp, scallops, salt and pepper and cook until seafood is just cooked, about 5 minutes.

While the sauce is cooking, add the penne to the boiling water and cook until tender, about 12 minutes. Drain the pasta and add it to the sauce. Toss together. Transfer the pasta and sauce to serving plates and garnish with chopped parsley.

Postcards from the Edge

Exercise Tip

Studies have shown that when you combine aerobic exercise with a weight-lifting program, you lose more body fat than people who engage only in aerobic activities.

Broccoli Raab

Broccoli rabe, raab, rappini or rape, is a vegetable that, despite its name, tastes nothing like broccoli. It is part of the cabbage family. This recipe is so good, we've been known to sit down with a plate of just this dish and a piece of good Italian bread. We feel like we're eating in a trattoria in Italy.

> **2 lb (1 kg) broccoli raab**
> **1 tbsp (15 mL) olive oil**
> **2 cloves garlic, minced**
> **salt and pepper to taste**
> **juice of 1/2 lemon**
> **6 lemon wedges for garnish**

Remove tough outer leaves of broccoli raab. Trim stems and peel lightly. Wash well and cut each stalk into thirds. Bring a large pot of water to boil. Add the broccoli raab and cook for 3 minutes. Drain and stop the cooking process by running under cold water. Drain again and pat dry.

Heat the oil in a large skillet over medium heat. Add the garlic and sauté for 2 minutes. Add the broccoli raab and season with salt and pepper. Cover skillet, turn heat to medium-low and cook for 10 minutes, stirring occasionally.

Remove from heat and sprinkle with lemon juice. Transfer to serving dishes and garnish each with a lemon wedge.

Cappuccino

Serves 6

Per serving:
Calories: 46
Fat: 0.2 g

Coffee lovers unite. We have come up with a cappuccino recipe that doesn't involve mortgaging the house to buy a specialized cappuccino machine. Here we beat warmed, skim milk in a blender to create that creamy, frothy topping for the espresso.

3 cups (750 mL) skim milk
3 cups (750 mL) strong, freshly brewed espresso
sugar to taste
6 whole cinnamon sticks

Heat the milk in a saucepan just to the scalding point. Transfer to a blender and beat until thick and frothy. Pour 1/2 cup (125 mL) of the espresso into each of 6 mugs. Top with 1/2 cup (125 mL) of the foamy milk. Serve with sugar and cinnamon sticks for stirring.

Makes about 50 biscotti

Per serving (1 biscuit):

Calories: 35
Fat: 0.7 g

Almond Biscotti

These cookies (we believe) were invented specifically for dunking. A real Italian treat is to sit in a café in the afternoon and dip this crunchy cookie into a glass of red wine. How's that for indulgence? These cookies are also nice with tea or coffee. Because they are twice-baked, they take a little longer to make than most cookies, but they store very well and at under a gram of fat, we say go for it.

> 2 tbsp (25 mL) soft margarine
> 2/3 cup (175 mL) sugar
> 1 tsp (5 mL) almond extract
> 3 large egg whites
> 2 cups (500 mL) all-purpose flour
> 2 tsp (10 mL) baking powder
> 1/4 tsp (1 mL) salt
> 1/4 cup (50 mL) toasted whole almonds (recipe
>   follows)

In a large bowl, cream together the margarine and sugar. Add the almond extract and egg whites and beat until fluffy. In a separate bowl, mix together the flour, baking powder, salt and almonds. Add the flour mixture to the egg white mixture and mix until you have a smooth dough. Cover the dough with plastic wrap and refrigerate for 30 minutes.

Preheat oven to 325°F (160°C). Coat a baking sheet with non-stick cooking spray and lightly dust it with flour, shaking off excess flour.

Remove the dough from refrigerator and divide it into 4 pieces. Shape each piece into a log about 1/2 inch (1 cm) thick and 12 inches (30 cm) long. Bake logs on the prepared pan for 30 minutes.

Remove baking sheet from oven and lower temperature to 250°F (120°C). When logs are cool enough to handle, cut the logs into 1/2-inch-thick (1 cm) slices diagonally, using a sharp knife. Place the slices back on baking sheet and bake for 15 to 20 minutes. Let cool completely before serving.

Toasted Almonds:

Spread almonds on ungreased baking sheet; bake at 350°F (180°C) for 10 to 15 minutes. Be careful they don't burn.

Postcards from the Edge

Just Remember

Slumps are like a soft bed. They're easy to get into and hard to get out of.
— Johnny Bench

Don't beat yourself up if you have a minor setback. Accept it and move on. Always remember to be kind and forgiving to yourself.

Chapter 7

Mediterranean Magic

Spanish and Portuguese Tapas Party

Sangria
Andalusian Gazpacho
Marinated Mushrooms and Artichoke Hearts
Spanish Seafood Stew
Portuguese Paprika Potatoes
Honey-Almond Cookies

Greek and Turkish Delights

Taramasalata (Fish Roe Dip)
Skordalia (Potato and Garlic Dip)
Chicken Souvlaki
Lemon Rice
Tsatsiki
Turkish Stuffed Eggplant
Lemon and Mint Sorbet with Ouzo

Middle East Feast

Falafel in Mini Pita
Lamb and Apricot Sultan Stew
Bulgur and Tabbouleh
Lebanese Carrot Salad
Dried Fruit Compote with Yogurt

The magic and the mystery that surrounds the Mediterranean intrigues us. We've never been, so we were curious to explore what this area of the world is all about. We decided to take a cruise from the Atlantic through the Mediterranean right to the Black Sea. Sounds exotic, doesn't it? We're definitely excited. As we researched this area, we discovered how many dishes from this area of the world we already love and gobble up. Unfortunately, we came across so many great dishes that we had to be very selective. We guarantee you won't be disappointed with our picks.

We begin our magical tour in Spain and Portugal with a Tapas (appetizers) Party. Who doesn't enjoy feasting on a variety of tapas? We certainly do. Put some Spanish music on the stereo while you set your buffet table. Dig into some Andalusian Gazpacho, Marinated Mushrooms and Artichoke Hearts, Spanish Seafood Stew and Paprika Potatoes. For those who must satisfy their sweet tooth, we've included Honey-Almond Cookies. Why don't you borrow a video on traditional Spanish dances from the library, grab a partner, pour the sangria and learn the flamenco? It's loads of fun and a great way to burn off those Spanish calories.

Next stops on our cruise are Greece and Turkey. In keeping with the Turkish favorite of yogurt, we've got a great selection of dips to choose from: Taramasalata, Skordalia and Tsatsiki. Perfect if served with pita bread, veggies or light crackers. Did we mention we have a fantastic recipe for stuffed eggplant? Olympians in training can find no fault with these great recipes. Low-fat and delicious — what more could you ask for? Of course, no Greek menu would be complete without a little bit of ouzo. But just a little bit, because, as we know from experience, too much ouzo makes one feel oozy in the morning.

Our Mediterranean cruise ends in the Middle East where we enjoy, among other dishes, Falafel and Tabbouleh. Both are perfect with toasted pita. Because we love them so much, they tend not to last too long around us. Fortunately, though, they are in line with all our dishes. They are scrumptiously low-fat, so we don't wake up feeling guilty the next morning.

Menu 1

Spanish and Portuguese Tapas Party

Sangria
Andalusian Gazpacho
Marinated Mushrooms and Artichoke Hearts
Spanish Seafood Stew
Portuguese Paprika Potatoes
Honey-Almond Cookies

Wine Suggestions

Torres Don Miguel, Spain

Serves 10

Per serving:
Calories: 146

Cocktails
Sangria

Sangria is a great warm weather treat. The fruit is like an added surprise at the bottom of the glass, flavorfully marinated in the wine. Our recipe calls for white wine, but if you prefer red wine, simply substitute 1 bottle of dry red wine.

> 2 cups (500 mL) sliced mixed fruit (peaches, nectarines, apples, melon, strawberries, oranges, lemons and limes)
> sugar to taste
> 1 bottle (3 to 4 cups/750 mL to 1 L) dry white wine
> 1 cup (250 mL) orange juice
> 1 cup (250 mL) grapefruit juice
> 1 1/2 cups (375 mL) soda water

Mix all ingredients except the soda water in a large jug. Stir to combine well. Refrigerate for 2 hours. Just before serving, add the soda water. Serve over ice in tall glasses, making sure to ladle some of the fruit into each glass.

Note: How much sugar you add depends on which fruit you use; some fruits are naturally sweeter than others.

Andalusian Gazpacho

Serves 4 to 6

Per serving:
Calories: 44
Fat: 0.3 g

Andalusia is a southern region in Spain. The temperatures are very warm there, and the cooking style of the region reflects that. Dishes are often light and simple, like this veggie-packed gazpacho.

2 slices dried bread, crusts removed
1 cup (250 mL) water
1 to 2 cloves garlic, chopped
1 small onion, chopped
1 cucumber, peeled, seeded and chopped
1 red or green bell pepper, seeded and chopped
2 lb (1 kg) tomatoes, cored, seeded and chopped
1 cup (250 mL) tomato juice
2 tbsp (25 mL) red wine vinegar
dash of hot pepper sauce
pinch of sugar
salt and pepper to taste

Garnishes:
2 slices of bread, cubed, baked on a baking sheet
    at 350°F (180°C) for 10 to 12 minutes
1/4 cup (50 mL) diced tomatoes
1/4 cup (50 mL) diced bell pepper
2 green onions, sliced

Soak the dried bread slices in water for 3 minutes. Remove the bread and squeeze out most of the moisture. In a food processor or blender, purée the soaked bread, garlic, onion, cucumber, bell pepper and tomatoes.

Mix together the tomato juice, vinegar, hot pepper sauce, sugar, salt and pepper and add it to the vegetables as you purée. You may have to purée the vegetables in batches, especially if using a blender.

Pour the soup into a tureen or large bowl and refrigerate for 1 hour. When ready to serve, ladle chilled gazpacho into bowls and pass around with the garnishes.

෨෨ ෨෨ ෨෨ ෨෨ ෨෨ ෨෨ ෨෨ ෨෨ ෨෨ ෨෨ ෨෨ ෨෨ ෨෨ ෨෨ ෨෨ ෨෨

Postcards from the Edge

In the Kitchen

Chickpeas are a great source of fiber and can be tossed into salads and soups or combined with rice, pasta, bulgur or couscous to make a complete protein.

Recipes often instruct you to salt eggplant before cooking in order to remove its bitterness. Blanching the eggplant slices in boiling water for 2 minutes will also do the trick.

According to Greek mythology, the Olympian goddess Athena brought the olive tree to Greece. Olive oil is a good choice over other oils and fats because it is rich in vitamin E and monounsaturated fats, which can reduce harmful levels of cholesterol in the bloodstream. It also has more flavor than many other oils, so a little goes a long way.

Marinated Mushrooms and Artichoke Hearts

Serves 6

Per serving:
Calories: 77
Fat: 2.0 g

In Spain, tapas — small, savory snacks — are usually served in the late afternoon with a glass of wine. They help to stave off hunger pangs until dinner, which is traditionally served late in the evening.

> 1 lb (500 g) mushrooms, cleaned
> 1 can (14 oz/398 mL) water-packed artichoke
>   hearts, drained
> 1/2 cup (125 mL) lemon juice
> 1/4 cup (50 mL) water
> 1 tbsp (15 mL) olive oil
> 2 tbsp (25 mL) red wine vinegar
> 2 cloves garlic, minced
> 1 tsp (5 mL) sugar
> 1 tsp (5 mL) dried basil
> 1 tsp (5 mL) dried thyme
> 1 bay leaf
> salt and pepper to taste

Halve or quarter the mushrooms if they are large. Quarter the artichoke hearts. Put the mushrooms and artichokes in a large bowl.

Put the remaining ingredients in a small saucepan, stirring to combine. Cook over medium heat until mixture is almost at the boiling point. Be careful not to boil. Simmer for 5 minutes, remove from heat and pour the mixture over the artichokes and mushrooms.

Let cool slightly, cover bowl and refrigerate for 8 to 12 hours, stirring occasionally. Remove the bay leaf before serving.

Serves 6

Per serving:

Calories: 141
Fat: 3.2 g

Spanish Seafood Stew

This bright, flavorful stew reflects the atmosphere of the Mediterranean. Served in an informal, friendly style with good friends on a warm afternoon, what more could you ask for? To serve as a tapas, place a small amount of each type of seafood in a small dish and top with a little of the broth. Add a slice of fresh bread to dip into the delicious juice.

> 2 tsp (10 mL) olive oil
> 2 large onions, sliced
> 2 cloves garlic, minced
> 1 tsp (5 mL) saffron threads
> 1/2 cup (125 mL) Spanish red wine
> 1/2 cup (125 mL) water
> 1 can (28 oz/796 mL) plum tomatoes, crushed,
>   with their juice
> 1/4 cup (50 mL) tomato paste
> 1 tbsp (15 mL) chopped fresh basil
> 2 tbsp (25 mL) grated orange zest
> 18 mussels, scrubbed, beards removed
> 9 large shrimp, shelled, deveined and halved
>   lengthwise
> 2 large squid, cleaned and cut in rings

Heat the oil in a non-stick saucepan over medium heat. Sauté the onion until softened, about 5 minutes. Add the garlic and sauté for 1 minute more. Add the saffron, wine and water and cook for 2 minutes. Add the tomatoes, tomato paste and basil. Bring to a boil, reduce heat to a simmer, cover and cook for 20 to 25 minutes.

Add the orange zest to the tomato mixture, stirring to combine. Add the mussels and cook for 3 minutes. Add the shrimp and squid and cook for 3 minutes longer. Cover saucepan and turn off heat. Let sit for 5 minutes before serving.

Postcards from the Edge

In the Kitchen

Yogurt is said to hold magical properties for longevity and protect us against disease and infection. Whether that's true or not, we don't know, but yogurt is a great source of calcium and makes a pleasing, nutritious between-meal snack. Look for the non-fat or low-fat versions and instead of buying it already flavored, try mixing in one of the following to plain yogurt:

1. 1 teaspoon (5 mL) instant coffee granules
2. 1 tablespoon (15 mL) jam
3. 1 teaspoon (5 mL) vanilla extract and 1 package artificial sweetener
4. Honey
5. Fresh fruit

Serves 6

Per serving:
Calories: 111
Fat: 3.0 g

Portuguese Paprika Potatoes

If you want to learn about Portuguese food, talk to our good friends Lynn and Roy Carreiro. Any of the food we've ever been served at their house has been absolutely unforgettable in its unique flavors or method of preparation. We borrowed from them this recipe for spicy potatoes and slimmed it down some. Here's to good friends and good food.

> 2 tsp (10 mL) olive oil
> 1 large onion, chopped
> 1 large tomato, seeded and chopped
> 2 cloves garlic, chopped
> 2 tbsp (25 mL) paprika
> 2 tbsp (25 mL) all-purpose flour
> 1 cup (250 mL) de-fatted chicken stock
> salt and pepper to taste
> 6 medium potatoes, peeled and sliced
> 2 tsp (10 mL) olive oil

Heat 2 teaspoons (10 mL) of oil in a large skillet over medium-low heat. Add the onion, tomato, garlic and paprika and cook for 8 to 10 minutes, stirring occasionally. Sprinkle the flour over the onion mixture and cook, stirring, for 2 minutes. Add the chicken stock, turn up heat and bring to a boil. Reduce heat and simmer until mixture has reduced to half, about 8 to 10 minutes.

Transfer the mixture to a food processor or blender and purée until smooth. Season with salt and pepper. Set the sauce aside.

Cover the potato slices with cold water in a large saucepan. Bring to a boil and cook potatoes until tender, about 10 minutes. Drain the potatoes and pat dry.

Heat the remaining 2 teaspoons of oil in a large skillet over medium heat. Add cooked potato slices and sauté, turning slices until brown and crisp on the outside. Transfer to serving plates and top with the reserved sauce.

Postcards from the Edge

Exercise Tip

We'd all like to be able to take a dip in the warm waters of the Mediterranean Sea, but until you can afford that luxury, how about swimming at your local community pool? It is a great low-impact way to workout and you can burn almost 300 calories an hour.

Makes 4 to 5 dozen cookies

Per serving (1 cookie):

Calories: 34
Fat: 1.2 g

Honey-Almond Cookies

These tasty cookies flavored with honey are a real treat. The combination of honey and almonds pops up all over the Mediterranean. We think it's a pretty good pairing, too. As they bake, the cloves inserted into the cookies will fill your home with the most appetizing aroma.

> 3 tbsp (50 mL) margarine
> 2 tbsp (25 mL) brown sugar
> 1/4 cup (50 mL) honey
> 1 egg, lightly beaten
> 2 tsp (10 mL) grated orange zest
> 1 tsp (5 mL) vanilla, almond or orange extract
> 1 1/2 cups (375 mL) all-purpose flour
> 1/4 tsp (1 mL) salt
> 1/4 tsp (1 mL) baking soda
> 1/2 cup (125 mL) coarsely chopped almonds
> 3 dozen whole cloves, or 1/8 tsp (0.5 mL) ground
>   cloves added to flour mixture

Preheat oven to 375°F (190°C). Lightly spray a baking sheet with non-stick cooking spray and set aside.

Mix the margarine, brown sugar and honey together. Add the egg, orange zest and vanilla extract.

In a second bowl, mix together the flour, salt, baking soda and ground cloves, if using. Add the flour mixture to the honey mixture and mix well. Stir in the almonds. Shape dough by level teaspoonsful (5 mL) into balls and place on the baking sheet. If using whole cloves, put one into each cookie at this point.

Bake until cookies are firm and just golden on the bottom, about 10 minutes. Remove to a rack to cool. Remove cloves before serving.

Menu 2

Greek and Turkish Delights

Taramasalata (Fish Roe Dip)
Skordalia (Potato and Garlic Dip)
Chicken Souvlaki
Lemon Rice
Tsatsiki
Turkish Stuffed Eggplant
Lemon and Mint Sorbet with Ouzo

Wine Suggestions

Apelia, Kourtakis, Greece

**Makes 2 cups
(500 mL)**

**Per serving
(2 tbsp/25 mL):**

**Calories: 44
Fat: 1.3 g**

Taramasalata
Fish Roe Dip

This unusual dip is made with a fish roe called tarama. While tarama is quite strong in flavor when on its own, it makes a delicate dip with a beautiful pale, pink color when blended with bread and yogurt.

> **5 slices dried, firm white bread, crusts removed**
> **1/2 cup (125 mL) skim milk or water**
> **2 jars (1.75 oz/50 g each) tarama (gray mullet or
>   carp roe), rinsed and drained**
> **1/4 cup (50 mL) onion, finely minced**
> **2 tbsp (25 mL) lemon juice**
> **1/2 cup (125 mL) plain non-fat yogurt**

Soak the bread slices in the milk briefly, drain and squeeze to remove excess milk. Reserve milk. Mix the tarama, onion and lemon juice in a food processor or blender until smooth. Alternately add the bread and reserved milk and blend until smooth. Put the mixture into a large bowl and fold in yogurt.

Serve in a serving dish. See the note on the following page for serving suggestions.

Skordalia Potato and Garlic Dip

Makes 2 cups
(500 mL)

Per serving
(2 tbsp/25 mL):
Calories: 36
Fat: 1.1 g

We love garlic. But eat a whole head of it? When garlic is roasted, its pungent flavor mellows and it becomes soft and creamy. We whip it up here with mashed potatoes and it becomes a dip to die for.

> 1 lb (500 g) boiling or baking potatoes
> 1 head garlic
> 2 tbsp (25 mL) red wine vinegar
> 1 tbsp (15 mL) olive oil
> salt to taste

If using boiling potatoes, peel, quarter and cook in a large saucepan with enough water to cover, until tender. Drain.

If using baking potatoes, wash and wrap in aluminum foil. Bake in a 400°F (200°C) oven until soft, about 45 minutes. Unwrap and remove pulp from skins.

Cut the top 1/4 inch (6 mm) off the garlic, leaving the head intact. Wrap the head in aluminum foil and bake in a 400°F (200°C) oven until very tender, about 30 to 40 minutes.

Mash the potatoes in a large bowl. Unwrap the garlic and squeeze the cloves into the bowl. Add the vinegar, oil and salt and blend until smooth. If the mixture is too thick, add a little hot water and keep mixing. If you want the dip to be quite smooth, blend in a food processor.

Note: Serve either of the dips with pita bread cut in wedges, at room temperature or toasted in the oven, along with a mixture of raw vegetables such as thickly sliced cucumber, cherry tomatoes and thinly sliced red, green or yellow peppers. For something different, try fennel. Thinly slice the bulb and soak in ice water until crisp. Drain and pat dry.

Postcards from the Edge

Living a Healthy Lifestyle

How could you possibly stop your feet from moving and your hips from swaying when you hear the sounds of a Spanish guitar and the passionate beat of Mediterranean music? Barb tells the story in our first book, *Armed and Dangerous*, of being a new mother and, in the middle of winter, putting some great music on the stereo and dancing, dancing, dancing in the living room as a way to fit exercise into her life. Well, she danced away 30 pounds and had a blast. Here are a few music picks we're sure will get you moving:

Gypsy Kings, *Greatest Hits*, Columbia/Sony
Various artists, *Flamenco — Fire and Grace*, Narada/Universal
Various artists, *Nuevo Flamenco*, Nascente/Kock International

Chicken Souvlaki

The smell of this marinade makes waiting to eat these kebobs almost torture. Lemon juice, cumin, bay leaves and oregano produce a heady aroma; you'll swear you're on one of the Greek isles. Greece has such a temperate climate that crops there thrive, and there is an abundance of fresh seafood in the Mediterranean Sea. No wonder Greeks are so full of life and celebration.

> 1 1/2 lb (750 g) boneless, skinless chicken breast
> 12 wooden skewers
> 1 onion, finely minced
> 2 cloves garlic, finely minced
> juice of 1 lemon
> 1 tsp (5 mL) cumin
> 2 bay leaves
> 1 tsp (5 mL) dried oregano, or 2 tbsp (25 mL)
>   chopped fresh oregano

Cut each chicken breast into 5 or 6 chunks and put in a large bowl or casserole dish. Soak the skewers in warm water while the chicken marinates.

Mix together the onion, garlic, lemon juice, cumin, bay leaves and oregano. Pour the marinade over the chicken; cover and refrigerate for 1 to 2 hours.

Remove the chicken from the marinade and thread onto the skewers. Grill skewers on a barbeque until chicken is cooked all the way through, about 7 minutes per side. You could also cook the skewers under the broiler, turning once during cooking time and watching that they don't burn.

Lemon Rice

This rice makes a perfect accompaniment to the Chicken Souvlaki. It is lightly flavored with lemon and has an added richness from being cooked in stock instead of water.

> 1 1/2 cups (375 mL) white basmati rice
> 3 cups (750 mL) de-fatted chicken stock
> 2 tbsp (25 mL) lemon juice
> 1/4 cup (50 mL) chopped fresh parsley

Rinse the rice in a sieve under cold running water and let drain. Put in a large saucepan with the chicken stock. Bring to a boil, cover and reduce heat to a simmer. Cook until rice has absorbed the liquid, about 15 minutes. Remove from heat and let stand, covered, for 5 minutes. Stir lemon juice and parsley into rice. Scoop a mound onto each serving plate and top with 2 of the souvlaki skewers.

Tsatsiki

Makes 3 cups
(750 mL)

Per serving:
(2 tbsp/25 mL):
Calories: 16
Fat: 0.1 g

Tsatsiki is a popular complement to Greek dishes. It is so popular that you can buy it ready-made in most grocery stores. Here we serve it as a sauce, but it also makes a nice dip for vegetables. The addition of mint makes it a refreshing condiment when served with spicy foods.

> 2 cucumbers, peeled, seeded and diced
> 2 cloves garlic, finely minced
> few drops hot pepper sauce
> salt to taste
> 1 1/2 cups (375 mL) Yogo Cheese (see recipe on
>   page 24)
> 2 tbsp (25 mL) chopped fresh mint

Mix all ingredients in a large bowl and refrigerate until well chilled.

If you prefer a smooth dip, mix the cucumber, garlic, hot pepper sauce, salt and Yogo Cheese in a food processor or blender until smooth. Turn into a bowl and stir in the mint. Serve with Chicken Souvlaki.

Serves 6

Per serving:

Calories: 86
Fat: 2.0 g

Turkish Stuffed Eggplant

With this recipe we delve into the elaborate spices of Turkey. Cinnamon and allspice are not commonly used in savory dishes in North America, but they turn this vegetable dish into something quite exotic. The skin of baby eggplants is tender enough that you don't have to peel them.

3 baby eggplants
salt
2 tsp (10 mL) olive oil
1 onion, chopped
1 clove garlic, minced
1 green pepper, seeded and chopped
1 lb (500 g) tomatoes, peeled and chopped
1 tbsp (15 mL) tomato paste
1 tsp (5 mL) cinnamon
1 tsp (5 mL) ground allspice
1 tsp (5 mL) paprika
salt and pepper to taste

Clockwise from top:
Taramasalata Fish Roe Dip (p. 194)
Skordalia Potato and Garlic Dip (p. 195)
Turkish Stuffed Eggplant (p. 200)
Chicken Souvlaki (p. 197)
Lemon Rice (p. 198)
Tsatsiki (p. 199)
Lemon and Mint Sorbet with Ouzo (p. 202)

Cut the eggplants in half lengthwise and sprinkle with a little salt. Place cut-side down in a colander in the sink and let drain for 1 hour. Rinse eggplants and pat dry. Place eggplants on a baking sheet lightly sprayed with non-stick cooking spray and broil until pierced easily with a fork, about 3 to 5 minutes per side. Remove from broiler and let stand.

Heat the oil in a large skillet over medium-high heat. Add the onion, garlic and green pepper and sauté until vegetables begin to soften, about 5 minutes. Add the tomatoes and sauté for 3 minutes more. Add the tomato paste, cinnamon, allspice, paprika, salt and pepper, stirring to combine. Turn heat down to medium and cook for 3 to 5 minutes.

Preheat oven to 400°F (200°C). Place the eggplants, cut side up, in a large casserole dish and, with a spoon, compact the eggplant flesh to make room for the stuffing. Spoon a little of the tomato mixture into each eggplant. Bake for 15 minutes.

Clockwise from top:
Perth Pumpkin Soup (p. 215)
Honey-Mustard Coleslaw (p. 221)
Barbie Shrimp on the Bar'Bie (p. 218)
Adelaide Angel Cake with Marshmallow Frosting (p. 222)
Emu Steak Sandwiches with Onion and Mushroom Sauce (p. 219)

Serves 6

Per serving:

Calories: 158
Fat: 0 g

Lemon and Mint Sorbet with Ouzo

We finish our Greek and Turkish meal with a light and refreshing sorbet flavored with tart lemon and mint. The final touch is a little Greek ouzo poured over the sorbet for a tasty licorice treat.

> **1 large bunch fresh mint, washed and stems removed**
> **grated zest of 1 large lemon**
> **1 cup (250 mL) sugar**
> **3 cups (750 mL) water**
> **1 cup (250 mL) lemon juice**
> **2 tbsp (30 mL) ouzo or sambuca (optional)**
> **fresh mint sprigs for garnish**

Combine the bunch of mint leaves, lemon zest, sugar and water in a small, heavy saucepan. Bring to a boil. Reduce heat and simmer until mixture is syrupy, about 10 minutes. Strain the liquid into a bowl and let cool completely.

When cool, add the lemon juice and stir to combine. Freeze the mixture in an ice cream maker according to manufacturer's directions or pour into a square baking pan and put in the freezer. Stir occasionally to keep the mixture smooth. Freeze until firm.

Scoop sorbet into serving dishes or parfait glasses and pour 1 teaspoon (5 mL) ouzo or sambuca over each just before serving. Garnish with fresh mint.

Menu 3

Middle East Feast

Falafel in Mini Pita
Lamb and Apricot Sultan Stew
Bulgur and Tabbouleh
Lebanese Carrot Salad
Dried Fruit Compote with Yogurt

Wine Suggestions

Domaine Cigogne, Morocco

Makes 12 falafel

Per serving (1 falafel):

**Calories: 142
Fat: 2.3 g**

Falafel in Mini Pita

We would like to thank our friend Dennis Lee for this great recipe. When we tested this recipe, we didn't realize only 1/4 cup (50 mL) bulgur was called for and cooked up a whole batch. Lucky we did. With so much left over to play with, we came up with a fabulous tabbouleh recipe that follows later in this menu.

> 1 1/4 cups (300 mL) canned chickpeas, rinsed and drained
> 1/4 cup (50 mL) cooked bulgur (cracked wheat)
> 1/4 tsp (1 mL) baking soda
> 2 cloves garlic, minced
> 1 tsp (5 mL) salt
> 3 tbsp (50 mL) all-purpose flour
> 1 egg white, lightly beaten
> 1/2 tsp (2 mL) coriander
> 1/2 tsp (2 mL) cumin
> 1/4 tsp (1 mL) turmeric
> 2 tsp (10 mL) vegetable oil
> 1 package (7 oz/200 g) mini pita breads
> 1 container (8 oz/227 g) Wendy and Barb's You Won't Believe This is Low-Fat Hummus
> 1 container (8 oz/227 g) Wendy and Barb's You Won't Believe This is Low-Fat Baba-Ghanouj

In a large bowl, mash the chickpeas with a fork or potato masher to a fine paste. Add bulgur, baking soda, garlic, salt, flour, egg white, coriander, cumin and turmeric. Mix together well. Shape mixture into balls the size of walnuts and flatten slightly.

Heat the oil in a large skillet and add the falafel. Cook over medium heat, turning once, until the falafel are golden brown on both sides. Remove to paper towels to drain slightly.

Cut the top 1/3 of each pita off and put one falafel inside each. Serve with Wendy and Barb's You Won't Believe This is Low-Fat Hummus and Baba-Ghanouj.

Lamb and Apricot Sultan Stew

The combination of meat and dried fruit is decidedly Middle Eastern. The countries of the Middle East are no strangers to masterful cooking. Stone tablets inscribed with recipes for a variety of soups and breads have been found dating back 4,000 years, to the time of the Mesopotamians.

> 2 tsp (10 mL) vegetable oil
> 1 1/2 lb (750 g) lean stewing lamb, cut in 1-inch cubes
> 2 large onions, chopped
> 3 large carrots, peeled and sliced
> 1 tsp (5 mL) cinnamon
> 1 tsp (5 mL) turmeric
> 1/4 tsp (1 mL) cumin
> 1/4 tsp (1 mL) coriander
> 1/2 cup (125 mL) dried apricots, soaked in water 1 hour, drained and quartered
> 2 tbsp (25 mL) lemon juice
> 2 cups (500 mL) water
> salt and pepper to taste
> 1/3 cup (75 mL) chopped fresh parsley

Heat the oil in a large saucepan over medium heat. Add the lamb and brown on all sides, stirring constantly. Remove lamb to a plate and set aside. Add the onion and carrots to the saucepan and sauté for 2 to 3 minutes, adding a little water if necessary to prevent the vegetables from burning.

Stir in the cinnamon, turmeric, cumin and coriander and sauté for 1 minute more. Add the lamb back to saucepan along with the apricots, lemon juice and water. Season with salt and pepper. Bring to a boil, reduce heat, cover and simmer until lamb and vegetables are tender, about 30 minutes. Just before serving, stir in the parsley. Serve with plain Bulgur or Tabbouleh (recipes follow).

Postcards from the Edge

Just Remember

If you don't know where you're going, you will probably end up somewhere else.
— Laurence J. Peter

Be specific about your goals and how you plan to reach them. It's easier to see progress when you know exactly what you want.

Bulgur and Tabbouleh

Each Middle Eastern country has its own recipe for tabbouleh. Made with bulgur, a nutty grain, and dressed up with tart lemon juice and fresh herbs, this interesting side dish is a nice change from the usual rice or potatoes served in North America.

Plain Bulgur:
1 cup (250 mL) bulgur (cracked wheat)
1 1/2 cups (375 mL) de-fatted chicken stock
salt and pepper to taste

Rinse the bulgur in a sieve under cold running water and drain. Place bulgur, stock, salt and pepper in a saucepan and bring to a boil. Reduce heat to low and simmer until all liquid has been absorbed, about 10 to 15 minutes. Remove from heat and let stand, covered, for an additional 10 to 15 minutes.

Tabbouleh:
1 cup (250 mL) bulgur
1 1/2 cups (375 mL) water
3 green onions, trimmed and sliced
3 medium tomatoes, cored, seeded and chopped
1/3 cup (75 mL) chopped fresh parsley
1/4 cup (50 mL) chopped fresh mint
2 tbsp (25 mL) lemon juice
2 tsp (10 mL) olive oil
salt and pepper to taste

Rinse bulgur in a sieve under cold running water, drain. Bring the bulgur and water to a boil in a saucepan. Cover, reduce heat and simmer until all liquid has been absorbed, about 10 to 15 minutes. Remove from heat and let sit, covered, for 10 minutes. Stir green onions, tomatoes, parsley and mint into bulgur, tossing to combine.

In a small bowl, whisk together the lemon juice, oil, salt and pepper. Pour the dressing over bulgur and toss to coat. Set aside until ready to serve. The tabbouleh should be served at room temperature.

Serves 6

Per serving:

Calories: 47
Fat: 1.0 g

Lebanese Carrot Salad

This slightly sweet carrot salad is made even more delightful by the addition of cumin and cinnamon. When used in small amounts, these two spices don't overpower the freshness of the carrots and herbs but will have your guests wondering just what your secret ingredient is.

> 5 carrots, peeled and cut into matchsticks
> 2 tbsp (25 mL) chopped fresh parsley
> 2 tbsp (25 mL) chopped fresh mint
> 1 tsp (5 mL) vegetable oil
> 2 tbsp (25 mL) lemon juice
> 1 tbsp (15 mL) honey
> 1 tsp (5 mL) cumin
> 1/8 tsp (0.5 mL) cinnamon
> salt and pepper to taste

Fill a medium-sized saucepan with water and bring to a boil. Blanch the carrot matchsticks for 2 minutes. Drain and refresh carrots under cold running water. Drain well and put in a large bowl. Add the parsley and mint.

In a smaller bowl, whisk together the oil, lemon juice, honey, cumin, cinnamon, salt and pepper. Pour the dressing over the carrots, tossing to coat. Serve at room temperature.

Dried Fruit Compote with Yogurt

Serves 6 to 8

Per serving:
Calories: 230
Fat: 0.5 g

It is likely cooks of the ancient Middle East who we should credit for the invention of yogurt. It is used in soups, sauces, vegetable dishes and desserts, including this one. Our dried fruit compote is exotically flavored with cardamom and orange flower water. You may have to visit a specialty food store to find the orange flower water, but it's well worth the effort.

> 1 cup (250 mL) sugar
> 1 cup (250 mL) water
> 1 tsp (5 mL) grated lemon zest
> 1/2 cup (125 mL) orange juice
> 1 cup (250 mL) dried apricots
> 1 cup (250 mL) pitted prunes
> 1 cup (250 mL) dried figs
> 1/2 cup (125 mL) raisins
> 1 cardamom pod
> 1 tsp (5 mL) orange flower water
> plain, non-fat yogurt

Combine the sugar, water and lemon zest in a medium-sized saucepan. Bring to a boil, then reduce heat and cook for about 3 minutes, stirring carefully until the sugar is dissolved. Add the orange juice, apricots, prunes, figs, raisins and cardamom. Cook over low heat until the fruit is soft, about 15 minutes. Remove from heat and allow to cool.

When compote is cool, stir in the orange flower water and remove the cardamom. Serve with a spoonful of plain non-fat yogurt.

Chapter 8

Aussies and Kiwis

Walkabout Dinner

Perth Pumpkin Soup
Damper Bread
Barbie Shrimp on the Bar'Bie
Emu Steak Sandwiches with Onion and Mushroom Sauce
Honey-Mustard Coleslaw
Adelaide Angel Cake with Marshmallow Frosting

New Zealand Spring Dinner

Baked Kiwi Mussels
Leg of Lamb with Mint Sauce
New Potatoes with Garlic Chives
Carrots and Snow Peas with Mandarin Sauce
Pavlova

G'day mates. Welcome to the land of kangaroos, surfers' paradise and the outback. With such a diverse land of savage deserts, majestic sunsets and spectacular coral reefs, we couldn't decide on which region to focus. Therefore, we've given you a Walkabout Dinner, offering you recipes from the north right down the coast to the south. When you're down and under, these recipes are a great pick me up.

How could we have an Australian spread without Barbie Shrimp (on the barbeque)? Ever tasted emu? Well, we've got a great recipe for Emu Steak Sandwiches with Onion and Mushroom Sauce that simply melts in your mouth. We even went so far as to adorn our Adelaide Angel Food Cake with a marshmallow frosting. Simply heaven. Even Crocodile Dundee wouldn't be able to resist an invitation to this Aussie spread. Who knows, he might even offer to be our tour guide when we venture into the heart of New Zealand.

We were always under the impression that New Zealand was close to Australia. Boy, were we wrong. It's more than 2,000 kilometers southwest of Sydney. To us, that means it's still classified as down under, even though it is definitely a country of its own. Complete with volcanoes, snow-capped ranges, fern-filled forests and subtropical beaches, New Zealand is blend of cultures, one that is neither Polynesian nor British. Simply put, it is purely New Zealand.

Apparently, the New Zealand national pastime is walking. How healthy. Wendy and Barb are very impressed. Similarly, most New Zealand dishes are healthy, hearty and filling. New Zealanders are famous for their lamb. We've provided you with a stunning leg of lamb recipe, topped with a scrumptious mint sauce. To accompany this mouth-watering dish, we've given you recipes for Baked Kiwi Mussels and New Potatoes with Garlic Chives. The national dessert, Pavlova, is a sinful concoction which we've given a Wendy and Barb makeover. Now, everyone can enjoy another guilt-free, low-fat treat. Between our Australian Walkabout Dinner and the national pastime of New Zealanders, our exercise suggestion in this chapter has to be walking. Put on those runners, grab that Walkman and walk until you drop.

Menu 1

Walkabout Dinner

Perth Pumpkin Soup
Damper Bread
Barbie Shrimp on the Bar'Bie
Emu Steak Sandwiches with Onion and Mushroom Sauce
Honey-Mustard Coleslaw
Adelaide Angel Cake with Marshmallow Frosting

Wine Suggestions

Wolf Blass Yellow Label, Cabernet Sauvignon, Australia

Perth Pumpkin Soup

Serves 6

Per serving:
Calories: 72
Fat: 0.3 g

Pumpkin soup is extremely popular in Australia. Even one of the name-brand soup companies distributes a canned version there. Take it from these two Sheilas, our smooth, creamy version is low-fat and fair dinkum.

> 1/4 cup (50 mL) vegetable stock
> 1 clove garlic, minced
> 1 large onion, chopped
> 1 cup (250 mL) chopped carrots
> 1/2 tsp (2 mL) ground ginger
> 1/2 tsp (2 mL) cinnamon
> 1/4 tsp (1 mL) ground nutmeg
> 1 can (14 oz/398 mL) cooked pumpkin or fresh
>   cooked pumpkin
> 4 cups (1 L) de-fatted chicken or vegetable stock
> 1 cup (250 mL) plain low-fat yogurt

Heat 1/4 cup (50 mL) stock in a large saucepan. Add the garlic, onion, carrots, ginger, cinnamon and nutmeg. Sauté over medium heat until vegetables are soft, about 10 minutes. Add the pumpkin and 4 cups stock and simmer over low heat, stirring occasionally, for 20 minutes.

Transfer the soup to a food processor or blender (you may have to do this in small batches) and purée. Return soup to saucepan and reheat over low heat. Stir in yogurt and stir until just heated through.

Damper Bread

This is a very easy bread to make. It is rumored to have been named for William Dampier, an English explorer in the days of the Australian colonies. Serve it with the Perth Pumpkin Soup or serve it topped with the grilled emu (recipe follows). Although this bread is traditionally cooked over open coals by the drovers in the outback, let's just stick to a conventional oven, shall we?

> 1/4 cup lukewarm water
> 1 package (1/4 oz/8 g) active dry yeast
> 1 tbsp (15 mL) sugar
> 3 cups (750 mL) all-purpose flour
> 2 tsp (10 mL) baking powder
> 1/2 tsp (2 mL) salt
> 3 tbsp (50 mL) vegetable shortening
> 1 cup (250 mL) buttermilk

Put the lukewarm water in a small bowl and sprinkle yeast over it. Stir in the sugar and set aside to let stand until mixture becomes foamy, about 5 minutes. In a large bowl, mix together the flour, baking powder and salt. Add the shortening and cut it into the flour mixture with a pastry blender or two knives until the mixture is crumbly. Stir in the yeast mixture and buttermilk and mix until the dough starts to form a ball.

Turn the dough out onto a lightly floured board and knead until smooth, about 2 minutes. Cover dough with waxed paper that has been sprayed with non-stick cooking spray and let sit for 10 minutes. Shape the dough into a round loaf about 8 inches (20 cm) in diameter. Place dough on a baking sheet that has been sprayed lightly with non-stick cooking spray. Cover again and let rise in a warm place free from drafts for 30 minutes. Preheat oven to 375°F (190°C). With a sharp knife or razor blade, cut an X in the top of the loaf. Bake loaf for 30 to 40 minutes. Cut bread in wedges or slices to serve.

Postcards from the Edge

In the Kitchen

Pumpkin boasts one of the highest amounts of Vitamin A of all vegetables, so don't wait for Thanksgiving to enjoy this power-packed vegetable. Choose small pumpkins for cooking since they are more tender and less stringy than the large ones. Save the big ones for carving jack-o'-lanterns.

Mussels are an inexpensive treat. One pound (500 g) of mussels is more than enough for two people and will probably cost you under five dollars. They are low in fat and high in protein and iron.

Barbie Shrimp on the Bar'Bie

Yes, yes, bad pun, we know, but how could we resist? With this big island being, of course, surrounded with water, seafood is a major mainstay of the Australian diet. The beer in the marinade imparts a wonderful taste to the shrimp. Just don't overcook them.

> 1 bottle of beer (preferably Fosters)
> 2 tbsp (25 mL) chopped fresh parsley
> 2 tbsp (25 mL) Dijon mustard
> 2 cloves garlic, minced
> 1 tsp (5 mL) whole peppercorns
> 1 tsp (5 mL) dried rosemary
> 1 bay leaf
> 1 1/2 lb (750 g) shrimp, in their shells, heads removed
> 8 wooden skewers, soaked for 30 minutes in warm water

Combine the beer, parsley, mustard, garlic, peppercorns, rosemary and bay leaf in a large glass mixing bowl. Mix well. Add the shrimp and toss to coat. Refrigerate for 30 minutes.

Remove the shrimp from marinade and thread on wooden skewers. Cook on a barbeque grill set about 4 inches (10 cm) above hot coals, for about 3 minutes per side. You could also broil the shrimp in the oven, for about 3 minutes per side, or just until shrimp are opaque.

Emu Steak Sandwiches with Onion and Mushroom Sauce

Yes, you read that right. Emu. The meat of these large birds is becoming more and more popular in cooking and is readily available in many areas. You can find a list of emu farms on the Internet or check with local specialty stores and restaurants. Emu meat tastes very similar to beef and is extremely lean and tender.

> 1 1/2 lb (750 g) tender emu or ostrich steak or sirloin or flank steak
> 8 crusty rolls, or 2 baguettes each cut in 4 pieces, for assembly
>
> Marinade:
> 1/2 cup (125 mL) dry red wine
> 1 large clove garlic, minced
> 1/2 tsp (2 mL) dried thyme
> 1/4 tsp (1 mL) black pepper
> 1 tsp (5 mL) Dijon mustard

With a fork, pierce steak deeply all over on both sides.

Combine wine, garlic, thyme, pepper and mustard in a large, flat, glass baking dish. Marinate the meat, covered, in refrigerator for 1 hour.

Remove the steak from marinade and pat dry, reserving marinade. Place steak on a barbeque grill that has been lightly sprayed with a non-stick cooking spray and cook about 4 inches (10 cm) above hot coals for 6 to 8 minutes per side (medium rare), or until desired doneness. Take steak off grill and allow to stand for 5 minutes. Slice steak very thinly against the grain and keep warm until assembly.

Onion and Mushroom Sauce:
2 tsp (10 mL) olive oil
2 large onions, thinly sliced
1/2 lb (250 g) mushrooms, cleaned and sliced
reserved marinade from steak

Heat oil in a skillet over medium heat. Add onion and sauté until they begin to soften, about 3 minutes. Add mushrooms and sauté for 3 minutes more. Add the reserved marinade, lower heat and simmer for 15 minutes.

To assemble sandwiches: Split rolls in half or, if using baguette, split each of the four pieces in half. Place sliced steak on bread and top with onion-mushroom sauce.

Honey-Mustard Coleslaw

This is a simple salad to serve with our emu sandwiches. It gets its creaminess from the non-fat sour cream and its kick of flavor from the gherkins, those little sweet pickles. The combination of red and white cabbage makes this a pretty slaw, too.

1 lb (500 g) white cabbage, thinly shredded
1 lb (500 g) red cabbage, thinly shredded
2 small zucchinis, shredded
2 small carrots, shredded
12 gherkin pickles, sliced
2 tbsp (25 mL) white wine vinegar
2 tbsp (25 mL) lemon juice
2 tbsp (25 mL) chopped fresh parsley
2 tbsp (25 mL) honey
2 tbsp (25 mL) Dijon mustard
1 cup (250 mL) non-fat sour cream
salt and pepper to taste

Combine the white and red cabbage, zucchinis, carrots and pickles in a large bowl. In a smaller bowl, combine the vinegar, lemon juice, parsley, honey, mustard and sour cream, stirring to blend thoroughly. Pour the dressing over vegetables and toss gently until combined. Add salt and pepper and toss again. Chill before serving.

Serves 12 to 14

Per serving (without frosting):

**Calories: 198
Fat: 0.4 g**

Adelaide Angel Cake with Marshmallow Frosting

Here's a bonzer treat and the crowning glory of our Walkabout Dinner. A mile-high, chocolate angel food cake. Angel food cake has been our saving grace on many occasions because it is made primarily with egg whites; even store-bought versions have very little fat. Our cake is a twist on the usual. It's flavored with cocoa and topped with marshmallow, but if you're short on time, simply buy an angel food cake and top it with fresh fruit and low-fat whipped topping for a quick and more-than-satisfying dessert.

> 1 cup (250 mL) cake and pastry flour
> 1/3 cup (75 mL) cocoa
> 1 3/4 (425 mL) cup sugar, divided
> 2 cups egg whites (about 14 large eggs) or 2
>   cartons of egg whites (1 cup/250 mL each), at
>   room temperature
> 1/4 tsp (1 mL) salt
> 1 1/2 tsp (7 mL) cream of tartar
> 1 tsp (5 mL) vanilla extract

Preheat oven to 375°F (190°C). Put the flour, cocoa and 3/4 cup (175 mL) of the sugar into a sieve over a medium-sized mixing bowl and, with a wooden spoon, stir until the ingredients are sifted into the bowl.

Beat the egg whites and salt in a large mixing bowl until foamy.

Add the cream of tartar and vanilla extract and beat until soft peaks form. Gradually beat in the remaining 1 cup (250 mL) sugar and continue beating until stiff peaks form. Fold the flour mixture into the egg whites (about 1/4 of the flour mixture at a time). Mix gently just until flour is incorporated. Do not overmix.

Turn the batter into an ungreased 10-inch (3 L) tube pan. Bake until a toothpick inserted in center comes out clean, about 35 to 45 minutes. Remove from oven, invert pan immediately onto a rack and allow to cool for 1 hour.

Loosen the cake from the pan gently and place on a cake plate. Frost with icing of your choice or dust with confectioners' sugar.

Marshmallow Frosting: Here's the trick: this is actually a ready-made topping. It is low in fat and makes a perfect icing for our cake. How's that for easy? You'll find marshmallow frosting in any grocery store, usually where peanut butter and jams are stocked.

Postcards from the Edge

Exercise Tip

You don't have to be an athlete to burn off some calories. Did you know that 1 hour of light kitchen work burns 138 calories? Now just put a little oomph in the vacuuming and dusting and you've got yourself a pretty good workout — and a clean house.

Menu 2

New Zealand Spring Dinner

Baked Kiwi Mussels
Leg of Lamb with Mint Sauce
New Potatoes with Garlic Chives
Carrots and Snow Peas with Mandarin Sauce
Pavlova

Wine Suggestions

Babich Marlborough, Sauvignon Blanc, New Zealand

Baked Kiwi Mussels

Serves 6

Per serving:
Calories: 99
Fat: 2.3 g

Kiwi mussels are a little different from the variety we usually find at our local fishmonger. They are very large and have beautiful pale green shells. You can find them in the frozen food section of most grocery stores (unfortunately, New Zealand is too far away to import them fresh). They are delicious.

> 24 New Zealand kiwi mussels or regular mussels
> 1 tsp (5 mL) olive oil
> 1 small onion, finely minced
> 1 clove garlic, finely minced
> 1 tomato, seeded and finely chopped
> 2 tbsp (25 mL) chopped fresh tarragon
> 1/2 cup (125 mL) dry white wine
> 1 tbsp (15 mL) lemon juice
> chopped fresh parsley for garnish

Kiwi mussels are usually packaged frozen on the half shell. If this is how you buy them, let them thaw in fridge, then place on the half shell in a large baking pan. Set aside while preparing the sauce. If using regular mussels, put in a stockpot with a small amount of water (1/4 cup/50 mL) set over high heat, cover and let mussels steam until opened, about 4 to 6 minutes. Remove from heat and when cool enough to handle, remove top shells and discard. Place mussels in half shell in baking pan.

Preheat oven to 400°F (200°C). In a small saucepan, heat the oil over medium heat. Add the onion and sauté for 3 minutes. Add the garlic and sauté for 1 minute. Add the tomato, tarragon, wine and lemon juice and bring to a boil. Lower heat to a simmer and cook for 5 minutes.

Remove from heat and spoon sauce over each mussel. Bake the mussels for 6 to 8 minutes. Serve immediately.

∽ ∽ ∽ ∽ ∽ ∽ ∽ ∽ ∽ ∽ ∽ ∽ ∽ ∽ ∽ ∽ ∽ ∽ ∽

Postcards from the Edge

Living a Healthy Lifestyle

The most popular sport in New Zealand is cricket, a game in which the ball, pitched by a bowler, is hit with a paddle-shaped bat. This very sporting game shows off the good manners and friendliness of New Zealanders. Cricket teams always sit down to eat together when they break for lunch. Could you imagine the Buffalo Bills and the San Francisco 49ers doing that?

Sometimes joining a recreational sports team is just the thing you need to get out of the house and get active. Most cities offer adult leagues in all sorts of sports. How about volleyball or badminton? Sports leagues are also a great way to meet people and have fun.

Leg of Lamb
with Mint Sauce

Serves 8

Per serving:
Calories: 283
Fat: 8.0 g

New Zealand exports its lamb all over the world. The lush country where the sheep graze makes for a tender, delicately flavored meat. Spring lamb is best since winter lamb is darker in color, stronger in flavor and tougher. Here we cook the lamb simply with a few fresh herbs and serve it up with pan juices and mint sauce.

> 1 3-lb (1.5 kg) leg of lamb
> 2 cloves garlic, slivered
> salt and pepper to taste
> 2 tbsp (25 mL) chopped fresh herbs (rosemary,
>   thyme, parsley)
> 1 cup (250 mL) red wine
> 1 cup (250 mL) beef stock

Preheat oven to 425°F (220°C).

Trim the lamb of excess fat. With a sharp knife, make small slits all over the leg and insert the slivers of garlic. Season the lamb with salt and pepper. Rub the herbs over the lamb. Place lamb in a roasting pan and pour in 1/2 cup (125 mL) of the wine and 1/2 cup (125 mL) of the stock.

Roast in the oven for 15 minutes. Reduce oven temperature to 350°F (180°C) and continue to roast, basting occasionally with the pan juices and adding the remaining 1/2 cup (125 mL) of wine and stock if necessary. Cook for 12 to 14 minutes per pound for medium rare or 16 to 18 minutes per pound for medium doneness.

Remove roasting pan from oven and let leg of lamb stand on a carving board for 10 minutes before carving.

Pour the pan juices into a de-fatting cup and let settle. Carefully pour de-fatted juice into a saucepan set over medium high heat and cook until reduced by half. Serve the juice and mint sauce (recipe follows) alongside the carved lamb.

Mint Sauce

**Makes about
1 cup (250 mL)**

**Per serving
(1 tsp/5 mL):**

**Calories: 12
Fat: 0 g**

If you grow mint in your garden, you know how it thrives. It springs up year after year, and before you know it, it has taken over the garden. This sauce is the ideal condiment to make in the summer when the mint is at its fullest and most flavorful. This sauce keeps very well for about a month, as the vinegar in it acts as a preservative.

> **1 cup (250 mL) fresh mint leaves**
> **1 cup (250 mL) white vinegar**
> **2 tbsp (25 mL) sugar**

Wash mint and pat dry. Stack 6 mint leaves, roll into a cigar shape and, with a sharp knife, chop as thinly as you can. Repeat with the remaining leaves.

Cook the chopped mint, vinegar and sugar in small saucepan over medium heat, stirring constantly until it boils. Reduce the heat to low and simmer for 15 minutes. This makes the mint concentrate. At this point, you can store the mixture in a glass jar in the refrigerator.

When ready to use, mix 1 tablespoon (15 mL) of mint concentrate with 1 teaspoon (5 mL) of vinegar; add 1 tablespoon (15 mL) chopped fresh mint and serve.

New Potatoes with Garlic Chives

Serves 6

Per serving:

Calories: 110
Fat: 1.9 g

This dish is best made with tiny new potatoes. Cooked whole and bursting with springtime flavor, they are a treat all on their own. Combining the potatoes with the chives sends them right over the top on the taste scale.

> 2 lb (1 kg) small new potatoes
> 1 tbsp (15 mL) margarine
> 2 tbsp (25 mL) snipped fresh garlic chives (or herb of your choice, such as mint, parsley or sage)

Scrub the potatoes. If they are very small, keep them whole. If medium-sized, halve them. Put potatoes in a large saucepan with just enough water to cover. Bring to a boil and cook until tender, about 20 minutes. Drain potatoes, return to saucepan and set over low heat to dry any remaining moisture.

Heat the margarine in a small saucepan. Add the chives and heat just until margarine has melted. Pour sauce over potatoes and toss to coat evenly. Serve hot.

Carrots and Snow Peas with Mandarin Sauce

Mandarin oranges give this dish a South Pacific accent. This is a simple side dish to make, so don't reserve it for company. Carrots are high in beta-carotene, Vitamin C and Vitamin A, so try to eat some either raw or cooked every day.

> 4 carrots, peeled and sliced
> 1 1/2 cups (375 mL) snow peas, ends trimmed
> and string removed
> 1 can (10 oz/284 mL) mandarin oranges, drained,
> juice reserved
> 1/4 cup (50 mL) orange juice
> 2 tbsp (25 mL) sherry
> 1 tbsp (15 mL) Dijon mustard
> 1 tbsp (15 mL) grated orange zest
> 1/4 tsp (1 mL) salt
> 1/4 tsp (1 mL) sugar

Bring a pot of water to the boil. Add the carrots and cook until almost tender, about 10 to 12 minutes. Add the snow peas and cook for 2 minutes. Drain and set aside.

In a small saucepan, mix the reserved mandarin juice with enough orange juice to make 1/2 cup (125 mL). Add the sherry, mustard, orange zest, salt and sugar and bring to a boil. Reduce heat to medium and cook until thickened slightly, about 5 minutes.

Put the vegetables in a bowl and add the mandarin oranges. Pour the sauce over and toss gently. Serve hot.

Pavlova

Here is a low-fat treat disguising itself as a decadent dessert. It is an old traditional recipe that we didn't even have to tweak too much to make low-fat. The base is made with egg whites, and we top it with fresh fruit and non-fat yogurt. Use whichever fruit you like, and just make sure it's the freshest you can find.

> 4 large egg whites
> 1/4 tsp (1 mL) salt
> 1 cup (250 mL) sugar
> 4 tsp (25 mL) cornstarch
> 1/2 tsp (2 mL) vanilla extract
> 2 tsp (10 mL) white vinegar

> Topping:
> 3 cups (750 mL) peeled, sliced kiwis or sliced fruit
>   of your choice
> 2 cups (500 mL) light whipped topping or non-fat
>   vanilla yogurt

Preheat oven to 250°F (120°C).

In a large clean bowl, beat the egg whites and salt together until soft peaks form.

In a small bowl, combine the sugar and cornstarch. Slowly add the sugar mixture to the egg whites, beating constantly until all of the sugar mixture is incorporated and the whites form stiff peaks. Beat in the vanilla extract and vinegar.

Lightly spray a large baking sheet with non-stick cooking spray and sprinkle with flour, shaking off excess. Pour the egg white mixture into the middle of the prepared pan and spread to form an 8-inch (20-cm) circle about 1 1/2 inches (4 cm) thick. Smooth the top with a spatula. Bake for 1 1/2 hours. Turn oven off and leave meringue in oven overnight.

To serve, place meringue on a serving plate. Spread the whipped topping over meringue and top with fresh fruit. Cut into wedges and serve.

Postcards from the Edge

Just Remember

A true vision takes on a life of its own.
— Greg Anderson

Make a plan for yourself. Write down exactly what you'd like to change in your life and how you think you can do this. Set realistic goals and update as you need.

Chapter 9

Asian Allure

Japanese Jewels

Miso Soup
Oysters with Daikon Relish
Norikami Sushi
Nigiri Sushi
Chicken Teriyaki
Bonsai Broccoli Trees
Rickshaw Rice
Orange Slices with Crystallized Ginger

Thailand Treasures

Hot and Sour Soup
Chicken Satay with Peanut Sauce
Sweet and Sour Cucumber
Shrimp Pad Thai
Mango Salad
Thai Iced Tea

Hop aboard the Wendy and Barb Orient Express to visit two of the most beautiful Asian destinations: Japan and Thailand. When we make these dishes, we love to do it all the way. We pull out the chopsticks, the grass mats, some pillows to kneel on and the coffee table for a buffet. You know from our previous book, *Spread Yourself Thin,* that we love to party, and Asian dining is one of our favorite themes. With these delectable dishes, we couldn't call this chapter anything other than Asian Allure.

The first stop on our Orient Express is Japan, the land where propriety is important and it is customary to bow upon meeting someone. However, a basic nod will suffice in most situations. Shoes are to be left at the door and only slippers are to be worn inside the home. We have a lot of fun with these Asian customs when we throw this party. Our guests don't mind once we serve our Miso Soup, Rickshaw Rice and Nigiri Sushi. In fact, they get right into it when we give them oshuboris (hot towels) to clean their hands.

Thailand possibly has the most diverse climate in Southeast Asia. Moreover, we think it boasts one of the world's most exciting cuisines. We certainly wouldn't turn down a round-trip ticket to this lush, green land of rice paddies. Unfortunately, such an opportunity hasn't come our way yet. That's okay, though; we've got our imaginations. It's definitely not hard to imagine being there when we dip into our tantalizing Hot and Sour Soup, Shrimp Pad Thai and Mango Salad, among other dishes. Interestingly, occasional rains in the dry season in Thailand are known as mango showers. Just imagine the land smelling sweet after such a shower. By the way, don't forget to try our Thai Iced Tea. It's very different from the typical North American version, but is so delightful you might find yourself serving it all of the time.

From the depths of the Orient, we've given you delicious, low-fat dishes that are sure to become your favorites. Who says you have to pay a fortune to experience Asian delights? Or that you have to pay a fortune to experience a new culture? We don't, and we do it every day in our kitchens.

Menu 1

Japanese Jewels

Miso Soup
Oysters with Daikon Relish
Norikami Sushi
Nigiri Sushi
Chicken Teriyaki
Bonsai Broccoli Trees
Rickshaw Rice
Orange Slices with Crystallized Ginger

Wine Suggestions

Sake

Sake is a clear, potent Asian wine. It is usually served warm out of a decanter. If you'd like to try to serve this in the traditional way, you can buy the decanter and small serving cups in Asian food stores. Different brands of sake are available, each with its own taste.

Serves 2

Per serving:

Calories: 106
Fat: 1.2 g

Miso Soup

This is a delicate soup to start your meal with. In most of Asia, all of the dishes are served at once, with the soup as a beverage as well as part of the meal. Try to use the dashi called for in this recipe, but if not, use a chicken stock that is low in both fat and sodium.

> 3 1/2 cups (850 mL) dashi (see note) or de-fatted
>   chicken stock
> 2 tbsp (25 mL) miso (see note)
> 2 cubes (1 inch/2.5 cm) bean curd (tofu)
> 1 green onion, sliced

Bring dashi to the boil. In a small bowl, mix 1/4 cup (50 mL) of the hot dashi with the miso until blended. Add miso mixture to the boiling dashi and stir well. Add the bean curd and onion and bring back to the boil. Cook for barely 1 minute longer. Remove from heat and ladle into 2 serving bowls.

Note: Dashi is a stock made from dried kelp or dried flaked fish. It can be purchased in a dried version. If you choose to use the dry, instant variety, bring 3 1/2 cups water (850 mL) to a boil, add 1 1/2 tablespoons (25 mL) dried dashi to the boiling water and simmer for 2 to 3 minutes before adding other ingredients.

Miso is a paste made from fermented soy beans and, sometimes, other grains. It is available at specialty or health food stores.

Oysters with Daikon Relish

Asian cuisine emphasizes the natural flavors of food. Here we have a unique appetizer of fresh oysters, perfection in a simple form. The relish accompanying the oysters is complementary in taste and appealing to the eye. Now, you know what they say about oysters and love, don't you? What could be more appropriate for this dinner for two?

> **4 large, fresh oysters**
>
> **Daikon Relish:**
> **2-inch (5-cm) piece daikon (white radish)**
> **1 dried hot red chili pepper**
> **1 green onion, sliced**
> **2 large lemon wedges**

Using an oyster knife or small, blunt knife, pry the oysters apart at the joint in the shells. Discard top shells. Cut the muscle holding each oyster to the bottom half of its shell, but leave each oyster in its bottom shell. This will be the serving container. Refrigerate oysters while preparing the relish.

Finely grate the daikon into a small bowl. Remove the seeds of the pepper and discard. Crumble the remainder of the pepper into the daikon and stir to combine.

Fill a shallow serving bowl with crushed ice. Place the oysters in their shells into the crushed ice, making sure they are sitting steady. Sprinkle the chopped onion on top of the oysters. Put a small amount of the daikon relish at the end of each shell. Serve lemon wedges alongside and squeeze a liberal amount over each oyster before eating.

Norikami Sushi

We have chosen smoked salmon for our sushi, making this sushi a very modern version. Traditional ingredients are fresh raw tuna, snapper, bream, bonito or kingfish. We offer you 2 recipes here. The first, Norikami Sushi, uses nori, a dried seaweed, to wrap the filling. The second, Nigiri Sushi, uses the salmon itself as the wrapper. Think of sushi as an eastern version of a sandwich. You can use any ingredient that you like for the filling in place of the salmon. An all-veggie sushi using wasabi, cucumber and mushrooms or blanched carrots for the filling is great.

As a time saver, the rice you make in this recipe will be divided between the sushi and a side dish for the Chicken Teriyaki.

> **Dressing:**
> 1 tbsp (15 mL) rice vinegar
> 1 tbsp (15 mL) sugar
> 1/2 tsp (2 mL) salt
> 2 tsp (10 mL) mirin (sweet rice wine) or dry
>   sherry

Combine all ingredients in a small saucepan and cook over low heat just until sugar dissolves.

Note: This dressing may be replaced with sushi vinegar, a store-bought dressing known as sushi su.

> **Rice:**
> 1 1/2 cups (375 mL) short-grain white rice
> 3 cups (750 mL) cold water

Rinse the rice several times in cold water and allow to drain for 30 minutes. Put rice and water into a saucepan. Quickly bring to a boil; cover and reduce heat to low. Simmer for 15 minutes without lifting the lid. Remove from heat and let stand, covered, for an additional 10 minutes to allow the rice to steam.

Transfer 1 cup (250 mL) of the cooked rice to a bowl, reserving the remainder to serve with the Chicken Teriyaki. Add sushi dressing to the rice in the bowl. Mix gently until combined.

Filling:
1 cup (250 mL) sushi rice
1 oz (30 g) smoked salmon, cut into 3 strips
1/2 green cucumber, lightly peeled (leave some
   green showing), cut lengthwise into strips
wasabi paste (see note)

Note: Wasabi is an extremely hot, green horseradish. You can buy it in Asian stores and many grocery stores either as a paste or dry powder. If using the dry form, mix a little of the powder with just enough water to make a paste. Allow to sit for 10 minutes. Bear in mind that a little goes a very long way.

To assemble:
1 sheet toasted nori
filling ingredients (above)
pickled ginger for garnish
Japanese dark soy sauce for garnish

Place the nori on a clean tea towel. Moisten your hands with cold water and spread the sushi rice evenly over 2/3 of the sheet, leaving about 1/2 inch (1 cm) at the end farthest away from you uncovered. In the middle of the sheet, spread a tiny bit of the wasabi, in a row. Place the salmon and cucumber strips on top of the wasabi, using just enough to make a single row from one edge of the nori to the other.

Using the tea towel and starting at the edge closest to you, roll the nori around the filling. Press firmly and evenly, pulling back the tea towel when necessary to form a tightly packed cylinder. Let the roll sit for 10 minutes, then slice with a sharp knife into 6 to 8 slices.

Serve the rolls on a tray with a garnish of wasabi, pickled ginger and Japanese dark soy sauce.

Postcards from the Edge

In the Kitchen

The cooking of Asia is centered around rice, vegetables and fruit, with meat and fats added in small amounts, more as a flavoring than a main part of the meal. We can learn a great lesson from this style of eating. It is healthy and satisfying at the same time.

Why not try using chopsticks when serving one of our Asian menus? They are designed to pick up food in small pieces and would also encourage you to eat slowly. When you eat slowly, the stomach has time to tell the brain it's full, which helps you not to overeat. Chopsticks are available in a lot of different styles and made from various materials and are easily found in specialty shops or houseware stores.

Nigiri Sushi

Makes 4 pieces

Per serving
(2 pieces):

Calories: 64.5
Fat: 0.9 g

Here is the second version of our sushi. This time, the salmon becomes the wrapper instead of the seaweed. This sushi looks like perfect pink golfballs. Strange comparison, we know, but you'll see.

> 1 oz (30 g) smoked salmon, cut on an angle into 4
>   very thin slices
> 1 tsp (5 mL) wasabi paste (see note on p. 239)
> 4 to 5 tbsp (50 to 75 mL) sushi rice
> 1/4 cucumber, lightly peeled, cut into 1/2-inch
>   (1-cm) strips
> pickled ginger for garnish
> Japanese dark soy sauce

Place 1 slice of the salmon on a clean tea towel. Spread a very small amount of wasabi on the salmon. Moisten your hands and place about 1 tablespoon (15 mL) of the rice on top of the salmon. Press 1 strip of cucumber into the rice, making sure it is shorter in width than the salmon. Bring the corners of the tea towel together, grasping it just above the rice mixture. Twist the tea towel, forming the sushi into a golfball shape. Unwrap the tea towel and place the ball (rough-side down) on a serving tray.

Serve with small bowls of wasabi, pickled ginger and Japanese dark soy sauce.

Serves 2

Per serving:

Calories: 253
Fat: 2.4 g

Chicken Teriyaki

Sweet mirin (rice wine) and sharp soy sauce make this chicken dish a true jewel of the Orient. Boneless, skinless chicken breasts keep the fat at bay. Slicing the chicken breasts before serving will make it easier to pick up with chopsticks (you did remember them, we hope).

Marinade:
1/2 cup (125 mL) soy sauce
1/2 cup (125 mL) mirin (sweet rice wine) or white
  wine
1/4 cup (50 mL) brown sugar
2 tbsp (25 mL) grated fresh ginger
4 cloves garlic, finely minced
4 green onions, finely chopped
2 boneless, skinless chicken breasts, 4 oz/125 g each

Glaze:
1/2 cup (125 mL) reserved marinade
1 tsp (5 mL) cornstarch

Mix all marinade ingredients together. Pour 1/2 cup (125 mL) of the marinade into a shallow bowl. Reserve the remaining marinade for the glaze.

Marinate the chicken breasts in a bowl in the refrigerator 30 minutes. Preheat broiler. Remove chicken breasts from marinade and pat dry. Broil chicken on a broiler pan about 5 inches (12 cm) from heat source, for 5 minutes. Turn the breasts over and broil until cooked through, about more 5 minutes.

While the chicken is cooking, combine the 1/2 cup (125 mL) of reserved marinade and the cornstarch in a small saucepan. Bring to a boil and cook and stir just until mixture thickens.

Slice each chicken breast into 1/2-inch (1 cm) thick slices on the diagonal. Transfer to a serving plate and drizzle glaze over each breast. Serve the remaining glaze in a sauce boat.

Postcards from the Edge

Living a Healthy Lifestyle

Plan your schedule so you'll know where you'll be if hunger strikes. That way, you can take the right kind of food with you or know where it's available, and you won't be tempted to turn into the drive-through for a quick fix.

Do not become a prisoner of bathroom scales or weight charts that are too general to accommodate the differences among people. Gauge your progress by the way your clothes fit, the way you feel or the fact someone complimented you on your appearance.

To keep motivated, read biographies of people who inspire you, whether it be for their humanity, for overcoming disabilities or for gaining personal or professional success.

Bonsai Broccoli Trees

We suggest you leave the broccoli in quite large pieces for this dish, for the aesthetic value; they will look like exquisite little trees. It is important not to overcook the broccoli. First, you want it to be bright green and crisp-tender, and second, overcooking depletes it of its vitamins and minerals. You want to get the most bang for your buck, don't you?

> **1/2 head broccoli**
> **2 cups (500 mL) water**
> **1/4 tsp (1 mL) salt**
> **1 lemon wedge**

Divide the broccoli, including a good part of the stalk, into 4 large flowerets. Lightly peel the outer skin of the stalk. Bring the water and salt to a boil in a saucepan. Add the broccoli flowerets and cook for 5 to 7 minutes. Don't overcook. The broccoli should be bright green and crisp-tender. Drain broccoli and squeeze the lemon wedge over it. Serve immediately.

Rickshaw Rice

Serves 4

Per serving:
Calories: 160
Fat: 0.3 g

Rice is the heart of Asian meals. Long-grain rice is preferred and is served either in a large serving dish or individual rice bowls. It is an important and revered staple of the Asian diet. Now is the time to use that leftover rice from the sushi recipe. If you don't have any reserved rice, here is a foolproof rice recipe.

> 2 cups (500 mL) cold water
> 1 cup (250 mL) long-grain rice

Bring the water and rice to a boil in an uncovered saucepan. Turn heat to low and cover. Simmer for 20 minutes without lifting the lid. Remove the saucepan from the heat and set aside, still covered, for 10 minutes. Just before serving, fluff the rice with a fork.

Serves 2

Per serving:
Calories: 70
Fat: 0.4 g

Orange Slices with Crystallized Ginger

Like us, everyone in the East likes sweets, but there, sweets are usually eaten as snacks, rather than as dessert. A simple dessert of fresh fruit is typical. Here we give you fresh, sweet oranges with the exotic hint of ginger. Now your sweetie won't be weighed down when showing appreciation for the delightful Asian meal you've prepared.

> **2 chilled oranges**
> **1 tbsp (15 mL) crystallized ginger (available at**
> **Asian food stores), finely chopped**
> **fresh mint sprigs for garnish**

Remove peel from oranges with a sharp knife, making sure to remove all of the white pith. Slice each orange into 1/4-inch (6-mm) slices and arrange on 2 serving plates. Pour any juice left over from slicing the oranges on top. Sprinkle a little of the crystallized ginger over each serving and garnish with fresh mint sprigs.

Menu 2

Thailand Treasures

Hot and Sour Soup
Chicken Satay with Peanut Sauce
Sweet and Sour Cucumber
Shrimp Pad Thai
Mango Salad
Thai Iced Tea

Wine Suggestions

Fetzer, Fumé Blanc, California

Serves 6

Per serving:

Calories: 170
Fat: 1.4 g

Hot and Sour Soup

Although this is a simple soup to make, it is jam-packed with flavor. Some of its ingredients are not common in our North American pantries but can easily be found in specialty food stores and even some grocery stores. It is important to get the right mix of hot and sour, so taste-test as you go.

1 cup (250 mL) dried mushrooms
1 cup (250 mL) boiling water
6 cups (1.5 L) de-fatted chicken stock
2 stalks lemon grass, cut in 1-inch (2.5-cm) pieces
1 piece (1 inch/2.5 cm) fresh ginger, peeled and
   sliced
2 cloves garlic, sliced
2 to 3 dried hot red chilies
2 tbsp (25 mL) vinegar
2 tbsp (25 mL) fish sauce (nam pla)
3 to 4 tbsp (50 mL) lime juice
2 tbsp (25 mL) chopped fresh cilantro
chopped fresh cilantro for garnish

Clockwise from top:
Orange Slices with Crystallized Ginger (p. 246)
Nigiri Sushi (p. 241)
Norikami Sushi (p. 238)
Rickshaw Rice (p. 245)
Chicken Teriyaki (p. 242)
Bonsai Broccoli Trees (p. 244)
Miso Soup (p. 236)
Oysters with Daikon Relish (p. 237)

Put the mushrooms in a bowl and pour boiling water over them. Let stand for 15 minutes. Drain and rinse. Remove the stems and discard. Slice tops.

Meanwhile, bring the stock, lemon grass, ginger, garlic, chilies, vinegar and fish sauce to a boil in a large saucepan. Reduce heat and simmer for 15 to 20 minutes. Strain the sauce, reserving liquid and discarding solids. Pour the stock back into saucepan. Add the sliced mushrooms and bring back to the boil, cooking for 2 to 3 minutes. Stir in the lime juice and cilantro. Remove from heat and taste-test for seasoning, adding more chilies (crushed), fish sauce or lime juice depending on just how hot or how sour you'd like the soup.

Serve in a tureen garnished with chopped cilantro.

Clockwise from top:
Dillyicious Cucumber Salad (p. 27)
Cedar Plank Salmon (p. 28)
Herbed Baked Potatoes (p. 30)
Flim Flam Fruit Flan (p. 31)
Veggie Kebobs (p. 29)
Canadian Coffee (p. 33)

Makes 12 skewers

Per serving (1 skewer):
Calories: 137
Fat: 1.9 g

Chicken Satay with Peanut Sauce

This is a great appetizer. With the addition of the peanut butter, this dipping sauce has the unmistakable flavor of Thai cuisine. You can find reduced-fat peanut butter in most grocery stores nowadays, which helps keep the fat content down.

4 boneless, skinless chicken breasts (4 oz/125 g each)
1 tbsp (15 mL) water
1 tbsp (15 mL) soy sauce
1 tbsp (15 mL) lime juice
1 tbsp (15 mL) grated fresh ginger
1 tbsp (15 mL) brown sugar
12 wooden skewers

Cut each chicken breast into 3 strips and put in a shallow glass dish. Mix together the water, soy sauce, lime juice, ginger and brown sugar. Pour marinade over the chicken strips. Cover dish and marinate in the refrigerator for 1 hour.

While chicken is marinating, soak the skewers in warm water for about 30 minutes. Remove chicken strips from marinade and thread each strip onto one skewer. Cook on a barbeque over medium-high heat 4 inches (10 cm) from heat for 5 to 6 minutes per side, or broil on the oven for the same amount of time per side. Serve on a platter with peanut sauce on the side.

Peanut Sauce:
1 tsp (5 mL) sesame oil
1 clove garlic, minced
1 cup (250 mL) de-fatted chicken stock
1/4 cup (50 mL) smooth, reduced-fat peanut
    butter
1 tbsp (15 mL) fish sauce (nam pla)
1 tbsp (15 mL) soy sauce
1 tbsp (15 mL) hoisin sauce
1 tbsp (15 mL) honey
2 tbsp (25 mL) rice wine vinegar
1/4 to 1/2 tsp (1 to 2 mL) chili paste or crushed
    red pepper flakes

Makes 1 3/4
cups (425 mL)

Per serving
(1 tbsp/15 mL):

Calories: **58**
Fat: **1.9 g**

Heat the sesame oil in a non-stick skillet over medium heat. Add the garlic and sauté for 1 minute. Add the stock and peanut butter and whisk until smooth. Add the fish sauce, soy sauce, hoisin sauce, honey, vinegar and chili paste. Bring sauce to a boil, then reduce heat to low and cook for 10 minutes. Remove from heat and transfer to a serving dish. Allow to cool to room temperature.

Serves 6

Per serving:
Calories: 34
Fat: 0.1 g

Sweet and Sour Cucumber

This is a wonderful condiment-style side dish to our meal. The coolness of the cucumber and the fire of the chili paste are a great combination.

> 1 English cucumber, lightly peeled and thinly
>   sliced
> 1 small red onion, chopped
> 1/4 cup (50 mL) boiling water
> 2 tbsp (25 mL) sugar
> 1/2 tsp (2 mL) salt
> 1/4 cup (50 mL) rice wine vinegar
> 1/4 to 1/2 tsp (1 to 2 mL) hot chili paste or red
>   pepper flakes
> 1 tbsp (15 mL) chopped fresh cilantro

Put the cucumber and onion in a medium-sized serving bowl. In a small bowl, pour the boiling water over the sugar and salt, stirring to dissolve. Add the vinegar, chili paste and cilantro and stir to combine. Pour dressing over vegetables, tossing to coat. Serve immediately.

Shrimp Pad Thai

The key ingredient in this dish is fish sauce, or nam pla. Despite its pungent taste and smell, we strongly recommend you use it in this dish. It adds such a distinct flavor, the Pad Thai just wouldn't be the same without it.

1 lb (500 mL) rice stick noodles or linguine
2 tsp (10 mL) vegetable oil
1 clove garlic, minced
1/2 lb (250 g) shrimp, shelled, deveined and
    halved
2 egg whites
2 tbsp (25 mL) fish sauce (nam pla)
1 tbsp (15 mL) ketchup
1 to 2 dried chilies, crushed
1 tbsp (15 mL) brown sugar
2 tbsp (25 mL) lime juice
2 tbsp (30 mL) finely chopped peanuts, divided in
    half
3 tbsp (50 mL) chopped fresh cilantro, divided
1 1/2 cups (375 mL) bean sprouts, divided

Soak the noodles in a large bowl of warm water for 20 minutes. Drain well and set aside. If using linguine, cook in boiling water just until tender.

Heat the oil in a large non-stick skillet over high heat. Add the garlic and sauté, stirring constantly for 1 minute. Add the shrimp and stir fry until shrimp just begin to turn pink, about 1 minute.

Turn heat down to medium. Push garlic and shrimp to one side of skillet and pour egg whites into skillet, stirring gently until just set. Add the drained noodles, fish sauce, ketchup, chilies, sugar, lime juice, 1 tablespoon (15 mL) of the peanuts, 2 tablespoons (25 mL) of the cilantro and 1 cup (250 mL) of the bean sprouts. Toss ingredients together for 3 minutes or until heated through. Turn mixture into a large serving bowl and garnish with the remaining peanuts, cilantro and bean sprouts.

Postcards from the Edge

Just Remember

What lies behind us and what lies before us are tiny matters compared to what lies within us.
— Oliver Wendell Holmes

You are a powerful force. The changes you want to make or have started to make in the quest for a healthier lifestyle are personal and completely up to you.

Mango Salad

Serves 6

Per serving:
Calories: 51
Fat: 0.3 g

Fresh fruit is the typical way to end a meal in Thailand. Delicious in its simplicity and a great way to cleanse the palate. Look for mangos that are soft to the touch and have some red-orange color to the skin.

> 3 large ripe mangos
> 3 tbsp (50 mL) lime juice
> 2 tbsp (25 mL) chopped fresh mint

Peel the mangos and cut away fruit from pit. Cut fruit into slices and arrange on a platter. Sprinkle with lime juice and garnish with fresh mint.

Thai Iced Tea

This Thai version of iced tea uses a tea that has a lovely reddish color and slight vanilla taste. It is mixed with sweetened condensed milk to turn it into a creamy treat.

> 1/2 cup (125 mL) Thai tea (powdered form,
>   available in Asian food stores)
> 4 cups (1 L) water
> 1 7-oz can (300 mL) sweetened condensed skim milk
> skim milk to taste

Put the tea in a coffee filter set in the container from your coffeemaker and place the container over a glass coffee pot. Bring water to a boil and pour it over the tea. After the water has dripped through the filter, pour the tea liquid into a second container and pour it through the tea powder again. Repeat this procedure 2 to 3 more times, until the tea is strong and has a deep reddish color.

Add the sweetened condensed milk and stir to combine. Allow the tea to cool to room temperature. Pour the tea into six tall glasses filled with ice. Thin the tea slightly with skim milk, stir and serve.

Chapter 10

A Scattering of Seeds

Quesadillas (Mexico)
Wonton Soup (China)
Scandinavian Scallop Salad (Scandinavia)
Russian Beet Salad (Russia)
Sauerbraten (Germany)
Potato Pancakes (Germany)
Moroccan Chicken Stew (Morocco)
Shrimp Curry (India)
Raita (India)
Kimchi (Pickled Korean Vegetables) (Korea)
Rodgrod (Denmark)
Almond Custard with Fruit (China)
Apple Bread Pudding (Canada)

Wine Suggestions

Sable View, Cabernet Sauvignon, South Africa

Pelee Island Gewürztraminer, Ontario

For Beer Lovers

Schneider Hefe Weisse, Germany

Whether you're on a safari in the jungles of Africa or about to do some serious partying in Mexico, this chapter of recipes gathered from all over the world will have you in a sweat and having fun in no time. Whatever your pleasure, whatever your taste, this chapter is jam-packed with delicious, and of course, low-fat dishes. These recipes are a must for any food lover. Imagine recipes such as Potato Pancakes and Sauerbraten from Germany, or Rodgrod from Denmark. Canada is known for its maple leaves, but how about its apples, loved the world over? When you try out our recipe for Apple Bread Pudding, you'll soon find out why we love the recipe so much. Don't forget about Scandinavia. We have a great recipe for Scallop Salad that we know you will enjoy. How about a Beet Salad, right from the heart of Russia?

We've got the ingredients for a great party, all you need are the invitations. The next time you want to throw a potluck and your friends ask what they should bring, assign each one of these recipes. Soon, you'll have the whole menu covered. Won't your friends be surprised when everyone shows up with dishes from around the world? These dishes are simple, to the point, but most of all, lots of fun. Even better, you don't have to worry about matching dinnerware. Who will notice? They'll be too into the spread on the table!

In this book, we wanted to transport you to the ends of the globe through the art of cooking. We hope we have succeeded in opening your eyes to a world of dishes that are so scrumptious and guilt-free to eat that they become part of your everyday menu. Don't be afraid to try new things, and always be open to ideas that may lead to a better, healthier you. Eat right, exercise right and you will live right. The Wendy and Barb Express is now landing. Please remain in your seats until we have made a complete stop. From our pilots, Wendy and Barb, we would like to say thank you for traveling with us. We hope you have enjoyed the ride. You're welcome back anytime.

**Makes 24
wedges**

**Per serving
(1 wedge):**

**Calories: 60
Fat: 1.3 g**

Quesadillas (Mexico)

We start our Around the World spread south of the border, in Mexico. We left out the huge amounts of cheese and switched to non-fat sour cream to make this hot little number more fitting to our low-fat spread. If you really want to turn up the heat, add some jalapeño peppers for an appetizer that will bite you back.

> **6 large flour tortillas**
> **2 large tomatoes, seeded and diced**
> **1 yellow pepper, seeded and diced**
> **1 red pepper, seeded and diced**
> **4 green onions, thinly sliced**
> **1/2 cup (125 mL) chopped fresh cilantro**
> **1/2 cup (125 mL) bottled salsa**
> **1/2 cup (125 mL) non-fat sour cream**
> **3/4 cup (175 mL) low-fat Monterey Jack cheese**

Heat a non-stick skillet over medium heat. Place one of the tortillas in the skillet and heat for about 2 minutes per side to make pliable. Place tortilla on a work surface and put a small amount of the tomatoes, peppers, onions, cilantro, salsa, sour cream and cheese on each. Fold the tortilla in half and press down lightly. Repeat this procedure with the remaining tortillas. Preheat oven to 400°F (200°C). Place folded tortillas on a baking sheet and bake for about 10 minutes or until cheese has melted and tortillas are lightly browned.

Remove from oven and let stand for 5 minutes before cutting each tortilla into 4 wedges. Serve with additional salsa for dipping.

Wonton Soup (China)

Serves 6

Per serving:
Calories: 103
Fat: 1.0 g

Once the wontons are prepared, this soup can be on the table in less than 10 minutes. Fast, simple cooking techniques are the art of Chinese cooking. Fresh foods and fast cooking in small amounts of oil add up to a lesson to be learned from this ancient and diverse country. With just a few additions to the spice and condiment cupboard, Chinese cuisine can be explored very easily in our North American kitchens.

> 1 lb (500 g) extra-lean ground turkey
> 1 clove garlic, minced
> 2 green onions, finely sliced
> 1 tbsp (15 mL) soy sauce
> 2 tsp (10 mL) sherry
> 2 tsp (10 mL) cornstarch
> salt and pepper to taste
> 1 package (1 lb/454 g) wonton wrappers
> 6 cups (1.5 L) de-fatted chicken stock (if using
>   canned, use 3 cans with enough water added to
>   make 6 cups/1.5 L)
> sliced green onions for garnish

Brown the turkey in a large skillet over medium-high heat, stirring constantly until cooked. Add the garlic and cook for 1 minute. Drain off any fat in the skillet. Add the two green onions, soy sauce, sherry, cornstarch, salt and pepper. Cook for 1 to 2 minutes. Remove from heat and let cool slightly.

Scoop about 1 teaspoon (5 mL) of the filling onto each of the wonton wrappers. Moisten the edges of the wrapper with water and fold over the filling to form a triangle. Press down on the filling slightly to make a dent in the middle. Fold the two widest corners of the triangle towards each other to meet over the filling and pinch the corners together. Repeat this procedure with the remaining wonton wrappers.

Bring the stock to a boil and add the wontons. Cook for 5 to 6 minutes uncovered. Serve immediately, garnished with the sliced green onions.

Postcards from the Edge

Living a Healthy Lifestyle

Drink your water. Dehydration can sneak up on you and make exercising very unpleasant by causing cramps and even heat exhaustion. Even when you aren't exercising, it is important to hydrate your body with pure water. The standard guideline is to drink eight 8-ounce (250 mL) glasses a day. This sounds like a lot, but it will make a world of difference in how you feel, how your skin looks and how your body performs.

Throughout the book we have waged war against fat, but we will say this: fat is essential to our bodies to aid in the absorption of fat-soluble vitamins like A, D, E and K, and to help our bodies function properly. But make your choices wisely. Choose unsaturated fats, which come from vegetable sources, and try to avoid saturated fats, which come from animal sources. Remember the magic number: try to keep daily fat calorie intake to under 30% of your total calories.

Scandinavian Scallop Salad

Serves 12

Per serving:
Calories: 89
Fat: 2.0 g

A light and refreshing salad from the land of the midnight sun (from June to July, in parts of Scandinavia, the sun never sets). Scandinavia is well known for its smorgasbord buffets of hot and cold dishes emphasizing fresh seafood. And, of course, it is home to the country that gave us Ikea.

10 to 12 cups (2.5 to 3 L) mixed salad greens,
    washed and torn
1 lb (500 g) mushrooms, cleaned and sliced
1 small cucumber, lightly peeled and thinly sliced
2 tbsp (25 mL) snipped fresh dill
1 1/2 lb (750 g) small bay scallops, cooked
fresh dill sprigs and lemon slices for garnish

Dressing:
1/4 cup lemon juice
2 tbsp vegetable oil
2 tbsp Dijon mustard
1 tbsp finely diced onion
salt and pepper to taste

Combine the lettuce, mushrooms, cucumber, dill and scallops in a large serving bowl. In a jar with a tight-fitting lid, combine all of the dressing ingredients and shake well to combine. Pour dressing over salad and toss to combine. Garnish with fresh dill sprigs and lemon slices.

Serves 6 to 8

Per serving:
Calories: 60
Fat: 1.6 g

Russian Beet Salad

From the land of the tzars, beautiful cathedrals and modern universities, we offer this colorful beet salad. Wendy and Barb think of Russia as a mysterious country, but what better way to learn about the history, culture and people of a country than through cooking? The trick we use when cooking beets is to leave the top bit of green on so that the red color doesn't seep out onto the countertop and you.

> **2 lb (1 kg) beets, washed and trimmed, leaving
>   about 1 inch of green stem**
> **1/4 cup (50 mL) vinegar**
> **2 tbsp (25 mL) water**
> **1 tbsp (15 mL) vegetable oil**
> **1 tbsp (15 mL) brown sugar**
> **2 tbsp (25 mL) onion, finely diced**
> **1 tsp (5 mL) horseradish**
> **1/4 tsp (1 mL) ground cloves**
> **salt and pepper to taste**

In a large saucepan, heat 3 quarts (3 L) of water to the boiling point. Add the beets and cook until tender when pierced with the tip of a knife, about 40 minutes.

Drain the beets and let sit until cool enough to handle. Peel beets and cut into 1/4-inch (6-mm) slices. Set the beets aside in a large bowl.

In a small bowl, whisk together the vinegar, water, oil, sugar, onion, horseradish, cloves, salt and pepper. Pour the dressing over the beets and let stand for 3 to 4 hours before serving, stirring occasionally.

Serves 12

Per serving:
Calories: 211
Fat: 6.2 g

Sauerbraten (Germany)

Although this isn't a difficult dish to prepare, it is time consuming. Begin preparing the recipe 2 days before you plan to serve it. The German people are known for their dedication to hard work, but they certainly know how to celebrate, too. From the Fasching Festival, which symbolizes the end of winter and the opening of the beer gardens, to the Munich Oktoberfest in the fall, we say *prosit* to everything Germany has to offer.

> 3 lb (1.5 kg) boneless beef rump roast, well
>   trimmed of fat
> 1 1/2 cups (375 mL) red wine
> 1 1/2 cups (375 mL) red wine vinegar
> 1/2 cup (125 mL) water
> 1 large onion, coarsely chopped
> 1 large carrot, coarsely chopped
> 10 whole cloves
> 10 whole black peppercorns
> 2 bay leaves
> 1 tsp (5 mL) caraway seeds
> 2 tsp (10 mL) vegetable oil
> 1/2 cup (125 mL) crushed gingersnaps
> chopped fresh parsley for garnish

Put the roast in a large resealable plastic bag and set in a casserole dish.

In a large saucepan, combine the wine, vinegar, water, onion, carrot, cloves, peppercorns, bay leaves and caraway seeds. Bring to a boil, reduce heat and simmer for 5 minutes. Remove from heat and allow to cool.

Pour the wine mixture into the bag with the meat and seal bag. Marinate the roast in the refrigerator for 48 hours, turning bag occasionally to keep the meat marinating evenly.

Remove the roast from the bag, reserving marinade. Pat the roast dry. Heat the oil in a large Dutch oven over medium heat. Add the roast and brown on all sides for 10 to 12 minutes. Add reserved marinade to Dutch oven and bring to a boil. Reduce heat, cover and simmer for 1 1/2 to 2 hours. Remove the roast to a platter and keep warm.

Strain the marinade into a de-fatting cup and discard any solids left in strainer. Pour de-fatted stock into a saucepan and bring to a boil. Stir in gingersnaps and reduce heat to low, cooking for 8 to 10 minutes. Slice roast and arrange on a serving platter; drizzle a little of the gingersnap sauce over top. Garnish with chopped fresh parsley.

Postcards from the Edge

Living a Healthy Lifestyle

Just because you're away on vacation is no excuse to give up all the good habits you've been learning. Why not rent a bicycle to tour around a new city or visit ancient ruins where there's certainly a lot of climbing involved? Plan more active holidays. You may come back more invigorated and refreshed than when you left.

Potato Pancakes (Germany)

Makes 12
pancakes

Per serving
(1 pancake):
Calories: 54
Fat: 0.2 g

These pancakes are best served hot with applesauce on the side.
We've included beer in the recipe since the Germans are famous
for their brewing. In the gasthof (local inn), ask for "helles" if you
want light beer and "dunkels" if you want dark beer.

> 4 large potatoes, peeled and shredded
> 4 green onions, finely sliced
> 2 tbsp (25 mL) chopped fresh parsley
> 1/4 tsp (1 mL) dried thyme
> 1/4 cup (50 mL) all-purpose flour
> 1/2 cup (125 mL) beer
> 1 egg white
> salt and pepper to taste
> applesauce (optional)

Put the potatoes in a clean tea towel, squeeze out any excess moisture and then put in a large bowl. Add green onions, parsley,
thyme, flour, beer, egg white, salt and pepper. Mix well.

Heat a non-stick skillet over medium-high heat. Spray lightly
with non-stick cooking spray. Scoop the batter into skillet in about
1/4-cup (50-mL) measurements for each pancake. Cook for 3 to 4
minutes per side or until golden brown. Transfer to a plate and
keep warm while cooking the remaining pancakes. If pancakes are
browning too quickly, turn heat down to medium, adding a little
more cooking spray as needed. Serve hot with a little applesauce
on the side if you like.

Serves 8

Per serving:
Calories: 305
Fat: 2.9 g

Moroccan Chicken Stew

The ports of Casablanca and Tangiers and the inland cities of Fez and Marrakech in Morocco, in northwest Africa, conjure up romantic images. Cinnamon, ginger, saffron and cumin make us think of far-off lands and give Moroccan cuisine its distinctive taste. This stew of chicken and couscous is the perfect one-pot meal for a buffet table or, with a light green salad, a terrific dinner.

> 2 tsp (10 mL) vegetable oil
> 4 boneless, skinless chicken breasts, cut in 1-inch
>   (2.5-cm) pieces
> 2 to 4 cloves garlic, minced
> 2 medium onions, thinly sliced
> 4 carrots, peeled and sliced
> 2 medium turnips, peeled and cut in large cubes
> 1 tsp (5 mL) cinnamon
> 1 tsp (5 mL) ground coriander
> 1/2 tsp (2 mL) saffron threads
> 1/2 tsp (2 mL) cumin
> salt and pepper to taste
> 1 1/2 cups (375 mL) de-fatted chicken stock
> 1 cup (250 mL) raisins
> 1 1/3 cups (325 mL) uncooked couscous
> chopped fresh cilantro for garnish

Heat the oil in a large saucepan over medium-high heat. Add the chicken and brown on all sides, stirring frequently, about 5 minutes. Add the garlic, onions, carrots and turnips and sauté for 3 minutes, adding a little water if saucepan gets too dry. Add the cinnamon, coriander, saffron, cumin, salt and pepper and sauté for 1 minute more.

Add the stock and raisins and bring to a boil. Cover saucepan, reduce heat and simmer for 10 to 15 minutes.

Add couscous, stirring to combine. Cover saucepan and remove from heat. Let stand for 5 minutes before fluffing couscous with a fork. Turn stew out onto a serving platter and sprinkle with cilantro.

Serves 6

Per serving:
Calories: 108
Fat: 2.4 g

Shrimp Curry (India)

Indian food is known for its diversity, largely because of the array of foods and spices from one region to the next. From Delhi to Madras, from Bombay to Calcutta, this is one exciting country. You can skydive, climb a mountain, go scuba diving or walk around the Taj Mahal. This curry dish hints at just some of the delights India has to offer.

2 tsp (10 mL) vegetable oil
1 onion, diced
1 clove garlic, minced
1 tbsp (15 mL) grated fresh ginger
1 tbsp (15 mL) curry powder
1 tsp (5 mL) cumin
1 tsp (5 mL) turmeric
pinch of cayenne
1 can (28 oz/796 mL) plum tomatoes, drained
    and crushed coarsely
1/2 cup (125 mL) canned light coconut milk
1 lb (500 g) shrimp, shelled, deveined and halved
    lengthwise
1/4 cup (50 mL) chopped fresh cilantro

Heat the oil in a large skillet over medium-high heat. Add the onion and sauté for 1 minute. Add the garlic and ginger and sauté for 1 minute more. Add the curry, cumin, turmeric and cayenne and cook, stirring, until spices have started releasing their aroma, about 1 to 2 minutes.

Add the tomatoes and coconut milk, stirring to combine. Bring to a boil, then lower heat so the sauce is barely simmering. Cook, stirring occasionally, for 10 to 15 minutes. Increase the heat to medium so sauce is bubbling, and add the shrimp and cilantro. Cook until shrimp are pink and just cooked, about 3 to 5 minutes. Serve the curry over hot rice accompanied by Raita (recipe follows).

ᏆᏆ ᏆᏆ ᏆᏆ ᏆᏆ ᏆᏆ ᏆᏆ ᏆᏆ ᏆᏆ ᏆᏆ ᏆᏆ ᏆᏆ ᏆᏆ ᏆᏆ ᏆᏆ ᏆᏆ ᏆᏆ ᏆᏆ

Postcards from the Edge

Entertaining

Entertaining doesn't have to be a lot of work or cost a lot of money. Keep in mind that the main point of entertaining is to be with people you like. Choose a menu that fits your budget and lifestyle. If you're short on time, why not choose to make one great recipe and buy ready-made side dishes from the store (low-fat versions, of course)? That way, you're not stressed, and you can spend more time with your friends rather than in the kitchen.

Makes 4 cups

**Per serving
(1/2 cup/
125 mL):**

**Calories: 61
Fat: 0.3 g**

Raita (India)

In India, raita is always served with spicy curry dishes to tame their fires. English cucumbers have fewer seeds than other types of cucumbers, so they don't need to be seeded if you use them in this recipe.

2 cucumbers, peeled, seeds removed, chopped
1 clove garlic, minced
2 tbsp (25 mL) chopped fresh parsley
1 tbsp (15 mL) chopped fresh mint
3 cups (750 mL) plain non-fat yogurt
1/2 tsp (2 mL) salt
1/2 tsp (2 mL) cumin

Combine all ingredients in a medium-sized bowl. Refrigerate for 1 hour to combine flavors. The cucumbers will release some of their juice while the mixture sits, so before serving, drain the raita and stir to combine ingredients again.

Kimchi
(Korean Pickled Vegetables)

Serves 8

Per serving:
Calories: 26
Fat: 0.1 g

These veggies have quite a bite, so tread lightly. You can easily adapt this recipe to your own taste by changing the number of chilies you use. This dish originated more than 1,000 years ago and was first made in an effort to preserve vegetables for the winter. Its spicy taste is said to stimulate the appetite.

> 1 1/2 cups (375 mL) sliced carrots
> 1 1/2 cups (375 mL) napa cabbage or celery
>   cabbage, cut in 1-inch (2.5 cm) pieces
> 1 1/2 cups (375 mL) cauliflower, broken
>   into flowerets
> 1 1/2 cups (375 mL) green beans, trimmed
>   and halved
> 1 cup (250 mL) white vinegar
> 1 1/4-inch (6-mm) piece of fresh ginger, sliced
> 1 dried chili, or 1/4 to 1/2 tsp (1 to 2 mL) red
>   pepper flakes
> 1 tsp (5 mL) sugar
> 1/2 tsp (2 mL) salt
> 1/2 tsp (2 mL) whole black peppercorns

Put the carrots, cabbage, cauliflower and green beans in a container with a tight-fitting lid. In a medium-sized bowl, mix the remaining ingredients, whisking to dissolve sugar and salt. Pour the mixture over the vegetables and stir to combine.

Cover the container and let stand at room temperature for 24 hours. Refrigerate for another 24 hours, shaking the container occasionally to mix contents. Serve in a small bowl as an accompaniment to meats and casseroles. Leftovers will keep in the refrigerator for up to a month.

@@ @@ @@ @@ @@ @@ @@ @@ @@ @@ @@ @@ @@ @@ @@ @@ @@ @@

Postcards from the Edge

Just Remember

Courage is very important. Like a muscle, it is strengthened by use.
— Ruth Gordon

You will ultimately reach your goal; the key is direction, not speed.
— Unknown

It takes courage to take charge of your life and make changes, believe us. You are worth fighting for. Your health is the most important thing in the world. Have faith and keep up the fight. A strong body and a strong mind go hand in hand.

Rodgrod (Denmark)

Serves 6

Per serving:
Calories: 82
Fat: 0.5 g

Everywhere you look in Denmark, you'll see crops and orchards. It is a very small country — you can tour the coast by ferry in less than 5 hours. Travel bugs like us, the Danish Vikings were exploring the world in the 8th century. This pudding is thickened with cornstarch instead of the eggs usually used in traditional puddings, making it a low-fat favorite of ours.

> 2 packages (10 oz/300 g each) frozen raspberries
> 1/4 cup (50 mL) cornstarch
> 2 tbsp (25 mL) sugar
> 1/2 cup (125 mL) cold water
> 1 tbsp (15 mL) lemon juice

Purée the berries in a blender. Pour berry mixture into a sieve over a saucepan and press the berries through to remove seeds.

In a small bowl, combine cornstarch, sugar and water and stir to blend. Pour cornstarch mixture into saucepan with berries. Bring mixture to a boil, stirring constantly. Boil for 1 minute, stirring constantly, then remove from heat. Add the lemon juice and stir to combine.

Divide the mixture equally among 6 serving bowls. Cover the bowls with plastic wrap and refrigerate for 2 to 4 hours. Serve with low-fat whipped topping.

Almond Custard with Fruit (China)

Lychee fruit are hard to stop eating once you've started. They're addictive, to say the least. This unusual dessert from China is very light after a heavy meal and also easy to make. Almonds have probably the least amount of fat of all nuts, and they add a nice crunch to this dessert.

> 1 1/2 cups (375 mL) cold water
> 2 envelopes (1/4 oz/8 g each) unflavored gelatin
> 1/3 cup (75 mL) sugar
> 1 cup (250 mL) skim milk
> 1 to 2 tsp (5 to 10 mL) almond extract
> 2 cans (19 oz/540 mL each) lychee fruit in syrup
> 2 cans (10 oz/284 mL) mandarin oranges
> 1/3 cup (75 mL) slivered almonds

Put the water in a medium-sized saucepan and sprinkle the gelatin over. Bring to a boil, stirring to dissolve the gelatin. Add the sugar and stir until sugar dissolves. Remove from heat and stir in the milk and almond extract. Pour mixture into a 9-inch (2 L) square baking pan and refrigerate until firm.

Cut the custard into square or diamond shapes. Place the fruit with syrup in serving bowls and arrange the custard pieces around it. Sprinkle slivered almonds over the fruit in each bowl.

Apple Bread Pudding (Canada)

Serves 16

Per serving:
Calories: 288
Fat: 3.9 g

We've taken you around the world and the last recipe we offer brings us back to where we started. Canada. Home sweet home. We finished the research for this book around Thanksgiving, and a trip to a local pick-your-own farm was the inspiration for this dessert. Standing in the orchards surrounded by trees heavy with Spartans and Ida Reds, walking with the family on a gorgeous October day, what could be more appropriate than developing a recipe that will remind you of those times whenever you smell it baking and whenever you serve it to the ones you love? It has now become a new favorite in our homes. We hope it will become one of yours, too.

> 1 cup (250 mL) packed brown sugar
> 1 tsp (5 mL) cinnamon
> 1/2 tsp (2 mL) nutmeg
> 1 tsp (5 mL) vanilla extract
> 1 egg
> 2 egg whites
> 2 1/2 cups (625 mL) unsweetened applesauce
> 3 cups (750 mL) skim milk
> 1/2 cup (125 mL) coarsely chopped pecans
> 3 medium apples, peeled, cored and chopped
> 6 cups (1.5 L) dried bread, cut in 1-inch (2.5 cm)
>   cubes

Preheat oven to 350°F (180°C).

In a large bowl, combine the sugar, cinnamon, nutmeg, vanilla extract, egg, egg whites and applesauce. Whisk to combine. Whisk in milk until mixture is fully incorporated. Add the pecans, apples and bread cubes. Push down on bread cubes and stir gently to combine. Let mixture sit for 10 minutes to allow the bread to absorb some of the liquid.

Spray a 9-inch (2.5 L) non-stick springform pan with non-stick cooking spray. Pour the batter into the pan. Bake until the pudding has set in the middle and a knife inserted into center comes out clean, about 60 minutes. Let pudding sit for 15 minutes, then release sides of pan. Cut pudding into thin wedges and serve with low-fat whipped topping, if desired.

Index

apple bread pudding, 277–278
apples, baked with Scotch whisky, 116
dried, compote with yogurt, 211
figs, 129
flim flam fruit flan, 31–32
ginger peaches and cream, 60
Malibu meringues, 76–77
mango-citrus salsa, 72–73
mango salad, 255
melon salad with anise cookies, 169–170
orange slices with crystallized ginger, 246
pavlova, 231–232
peaches, amaretti-stuffed, 161
rodgrod, 275
saskatoon berries with fromage blanc, 39
star fruit, 84
star fruit salsa, 85
strawberry jam, fresh, 108
tropical fruit salad, 98
wild blueberries with maple cream, 25

G

Galway Gingerbread Cake, 124–125
Garlic
to peel, 165
and potato dip, 195–196
Gazpacho, Andalusian, 185–186
Ginger Peaches and Cream, 60
Gingerbread cake, Galway, 124–125
Grilled Lobster with Tri-Dipping Sauces, 13–15

H

Ham Topping (for sandwiches), 105
Hang Ten Tuna with Mango-Citrus Salsa, 72–73
Herbed Baked Potatoes, 30
Herbed Yogo Cheese, 23–24
Herbes de Provence, 146
Honey-Almond Cookies, 192
Honey-Mustard Coleslaw, 221
Hoppin' John Salad, 67
Hot and Sour Soup, 248–249

J

Jerk Chicken with Star Fruit Salsa, 84–85

K

Kale, 83
and rice, calabaza with, 86
Kebobs
chicken souvlaki, 197
veggie, 29
Kimchi, 273–274
Kirsch, 129
Korean Pickled Vegetables, 273–274

L

Lamb
leg, with mint sauce, 227–228
Tony Bennett's Irish stew, 119–120
Lamb and Apricot Sultan Stew, 206–207
Lavender, 146
Lebanese Carrot Salad, 210
Leek(s)
Cork colcannon, 121
creamy soup, 112

Leg of Lamb with Mint Sauce, 227–228
Legumes
Brazilian black bean salad, 91–92
chickpeas, 186
falafel in mini pita, 204–205
Hoppin' John salad, 67
Lemon and Mint Sorbet with Ouzo, 202
Lemon Dill Dip, 14
Lemon rice, 198
Lobster, grilled, with tri-dipping sauces, 13–15

M

Malibu Meringues, 76–77
Mama Marranca's Minestrone, 164–165
Mandarin Sauce, 230
Mango-Citrus Salsa, 72–73
Mango Salad, 255
Maple syrup
Canadian coffee, 33
wild blueberries with maple cream, 25
Marinated Green Beans, 96
Marinated Mushrooms and Artichoke Hearts, 187
Melon Salad with Anise Cookies, 169–170
Mesclun and Orange Salad, 147
Milanese Risotto, 158
Minestrone, Mama Marranca's, 164–165
Mint Sauce, 228
Miso Soup, 236
Moroccan Chicken Stew, 268–269
Muffins
Carolina cornmeal, 66
princess pear brioche, 109
Mushroom and Onion Sauce, 220
Mushroom Ceviche, 90

"You Won't Believe This Is Low-Fat" Product List

Hummus
Spicy Hummus
Baba Ghanouj
Bruschetta
Original Cream Cheese
Tri-Peppercorn Cream Cheese
Garlic and Fine Herb Cream Cheese
Apple and Cinnamon Cream Cheese
Vegetable Spread
Spinach Spread

Available at grocery stores throughout Canada